THE LAST EDWARDIAN AT NO. 10

THE LAST EDWARDIAN AT NO. 10

An Impression of Harold Macmillan

George Hutchinson

QUARTET BOOKS
LONDON MELBOURNE NEW YORK

To Pamela

First published by Quartet Books Limited 1980
A member of the Namara Group
27 Goodge Street, London W1P 1FD

Copyright © 1980 by George Hutchinson

ISBN 0 7043 2232 3

The publishers would like to thank the following
for permission to reproduce illustrations: The
Macmillan Family Archive (pictures nos. 1, 2, 3,
6, 8, 26); The War Office (no. 4); Imperial War
Museum (no. 5); Sport and General (nos. 7, 13);
British Information Service (no. 9); Central Office
of Information (no. 10); Keystone Press Agency
(no. 11); Camera Press (nos. 12, 17–25); Popper-
foto (no. 14); Douglas Weaver (no. 15); Photo
Press (no. 16).

Photoset, printed and bound
in Great Britain by
REDWOOD BURN LIMITED
Trowbridge & Esher

Introduction

Born a late Victorian, Harold Macmillan entered
the Edwardian era as a young boy. He was seven
when the old Queen died after an almost lifelong
reign. In manner, appearance, sentiment and
culture he reflects the quintessential Edwardian to
this day. Many of his tastes, inclinations and sympathies are those of the Edwardian society in which
he grew up. Some of his sorrows are those of the
survivors of the Edwardian generation decimated
on the battlefields of France. He is an Edwardian
who has far outlived most of his contemporaries.

A year or two ago, he contributed a foreword to
a little book of Edwardian pictures.[1] 'Why do we
look back with such indulgent nostalgia upon the
brief era of Edward the Seventh?' he asked. 'For
those of us who remember it, the Edwardian
summer was an Indian summer, the last "warm
spell" of the Victorian Pax Britannica before the

First World War engulfed us all and almost destroyed our generation. Historians, with their unlovable habit of seeing in retrospect what we could not see at the time, may say that it was an age built upon illusions, and it is true that our fond belief that our world, no doubt with continual if small changes for the better, would last for ever was the greatest of illusions. But the peace and the sense of security which we enjoyed were not illusions. We really were at peace, we really did feel secure in the world . . . The darker side of Edwardian England cast but the smallest of shadows upon the general sense of confidence and peace.'

The phrase 'confidence and peace' may be said to express the aspirations of a lifetime. From first to last he has tried to imbue his fellow countrymen with a spirit of national confidence, and by example to foster, encourage and sustain it, while the dread of war – the memory of war – has inspired in him an equally unyielding commitment to the preservation of peace.

But if he often looks back, with feelings of pride, appreciation and regret, to the happier days of his childhood and early youth, he has never surrendered to despair for the future. Whatever his disappointments (and he has suffered a good many), he has not succumbed to pessimism. On the contrary, he has continued to look forward with hope: hope founded upon the insights of a cultivated mind and the instincts of a compassionate nature fortified by an understanding of the lessons of history and an ability to distinguish between the greater and the lesser objectives in the political direction of human affairs: in sum, one might say, the attributes – the equipment – of statesmanship.

Within the compass of this book, a selective but I

hope representative mélange extracted from an overflowing canvas, I have tried to convey some sense of his essential goals and an impression of his character, his temperament, his philosophy, the flavour of his conversation, the geniality of his company.

Although I cannot expect him to agree with everything that I have written, my affection for Mr Macmillan will be apparent to the reader from the outset. I owe him profound thanks for many acts of friendship, and again salute him.

May 1979   G.H.

Chapter 1

Since his resignation in October 1963, after six years and nine months as Prime Minister in a period of rapid social transition and political change, Harold Macmillan's reputation has fluctuated and varied in accordance with individual judgements of his record, his legacy and the consequences that may arguably be attributed to them. One ascription is seldom in dispute, however: he is remembered as an uncommonly *interesting* Prime Minister – no sobersides, no dullard, but stimulating, frequently bold. In some aspects a traditionalist, he was in others an innovator of radical impulse. Measured against subsequent experience, a number of his policies have become even more contentious or debatable than they were when he introduced them.

Thus it is said by some of his critics, pronouncing in comfortable retrospect, that in economic management he was a Keynesian of a dangerous order, a growth merchant, a reckless expansionist, an old inflationist with more than a touch of the collectivist in his make-up. Furthermore, it is said that he hustled us out of Africa and into Europe, precipitately abandoning one continent and too readily embracing the other. Again, he is accused of contributing to our moral decline by introducing Premium Bonds while Chancellor of the Exchequer and then accelerating our fall when Prime Minister by extolling 'the affluent society' as an ideal – 'You've never had it so good', and all that.

These charges are not without some substance. He *was* a Keynesian by disposition (not to mention early friendship). He was by temperament and conviction an expansionist, a spender, with no great propensity for retrenchment in the public sphere. By reason of his own proclivities, he did, after all, succeed in losing two Chancellors: Peter Thorneycroft by resignation, Selwyn Lloyd by dismissal. In principle, he was not averse to State regulation of the economy, with its accompanying extension of bureaucratic intrusion: this he had demonstrated many years earlier in his book *The Middle Way*.[2] In Africa he did undoubtedly encourage what some would call the hasty surrender of European influence and authority in favour of independence – or 'black power'. He did turn to Europe after weighing up the Commonwealth, relating his assessment to the domestic economy and concluding – perhaps over-eagerly – that our future prosperity, if we were to enjoy any at all, lay inescapably in association with the EEC.

While these may be facets of the larger truth, there

are others, some of them much more favourable to Macmillan. Horace Walpole observed sweepingly: 'It is one of the bad effects of living in one's own time that one never knows the truth of it till one is dead.' Walpole was extravagant.

What we do know is that when Macmillan assumed office the country was deeply divided and dejected, and that he quickly succeeded in generating a fresh spirit of hope and confidence. In the wake of Suez, the nation was disgruntled and downcast, and he transformed the mood. A sluggish economy was revitalized and sharpened to such an extent that, at least for a while, living standards rose rapidly. Many – indeed millions – enjoyed an unaccustomed sense of material well-being, and took to their new condition with enthusiasm. It is not too much to say that this was an interlude of unfamiliar domestic comfort as distinct from familiar domestic hardship.

Abroad, Macmillan repaired our relations with the United States. He was active and consistent in his efforts towards a better understanding with the Soviet Union, permissibly conciliatory when the occasion seemed to justify that attitude, but never compliant. As to his African policy, those who advocated immediate or early independence will no doubt continue to commend his 'wind of change' speech and the underlying outlook, just as its opponents will continue to decry it. Likewise with Europe: those who support British membership of the EEC must be expected to defend his initiative in trying to secure admission, while others look back disapprovingly.

Controversial in office, Macmillan will remain

controversial in retrospect. As Prime Minister he was, after all, the product of controversy of a character previously unknown to Britain in the present century and scarcely conceivable in the future.

He became Prime Minister in circumstances of a darkly dramatic nature – in what seemed the politically ruinous aftermath of Suez, which destroyed his predecessor, Anthony Eden, and threatened the survival of the Conservative Government. Yet within three years of his appointment the Tories had succeeded in living down the Suez policy and its attendant humiliations, had regained their authority and sealed their recovery by one of the most remarkable election victories of modern times.

Just as he entered No. 10 Downing Street in drama, so he departed; and the years between were themselves filled with drama, some welcome, some unwelcome. This was a period compounded of exhilaration and tranquillity, of change accompanied by a reassuring impression of stability; a period marked by advance in general social conditions and encompassing a revolution – active or incipient – in public tastes, attitudes, morals. Inflation on the destructive scale that we have since experienced was unknown, its beginnings all too seldom perceived; the more disturbing pressures of immigration were not yet upon us, nor were those of the movement towards devolution. The 'permissive society' was coming into being. The Cold War had not yet been succeeded by the age of 'détente', carrying a menace of its own.

As a nation, we were in clover – or so it may have seemed for much of the Macmillan premiership. He headed a government rich in individual talents and accomplishments of a quality no longer present in

Parliament in such abundance. Its members did not always attain their aims and purposes, but a good many of them were undeniably distinguished in their own right. This was probably the last of the classic or 'aristocratic' Tory ministries. Macmillan was the last Edwardian at No. 10.

In retirement, he remains unique in national life. After relinquishing office, he remarked: 'It has always seemed to me more artistic, when the curtain falls on the last performance, to accept the inevitable *E finita la Commedia*. It is tempting, perhaps, but unrewarding to hang about the green-room after final retirement from the stage.' He is no recluse, however, and although removed from the hurly-burly of parliamentary affairs he retains a sharp and critical interest.

Not surprisingly, he regrets what he considers the prevailing lack of political culture. 'Even young academics are ill-informed except on their own subject,' he was saying to me not long ago. 'Their predecessors were so much broader. Keynes was an economist by mistake: he was a humanist, a classical scholar. He wasn't like the modern economists . . . Of course we used to call it political economy. Political economy – Adam Smith – was about chaps, about people.'

It is probably true, and not in the least degree disparaging, to say that Macmillan is a nominal Tory, at heart a Whig, like some of the best of Conservatives. He has always been capable of detachment from party dogma, doctrine and prejudice. At eighty-five, he is still a fascinating influence, not

only as the most distinguished of our elder statesmen, but as the head of one of the few political
families still in business, so to speak – a family with
many ramifications, many alliances, parliamentary
and otherwise.

He seldom speaks in public nowadays: 'You're
either on the stage or off it. I don't want to make
political pronouncements. What could I do in the
House of Lords? I would have to make a speech
from time to time, say what I thought, or else not
attend – in which case there's no point in belonging
to it.' Yet he does make political speeches on occasion, however rarely, as in the referendum campaign
in the summer of 1975, when he spoke in support
of his son-in-law, Julian Amery, and the European
policy of which he himself was author. In retirement he has written abundantly: his memoirs,[3]
amounting to more than two million words in six
volumes; his subsequent book of essays, *The Past
Masters*.[4] His occasional performances on television
are generally accounted superb. Best of all, he pro-
nounces in private, to the everlasting enjoyment of
his friends and intimates. Thus he continues to
influence informed opinion, certainly within the
Tory Party, rather more than is commonly realized.

There is little of significance in national life that
escapes his notice. He is alert to events, knowledge-
able and responsive, with his wry and witty comments on the passing scene. He is not a cynic, but a
sceptic. As a conversationalist he has few equals: he
is both entertaining and instructive, ranging and
roaming from the immediate present to the remote
past, as fancy takes him. At one moment he is
discussing, say, Harold Wilson, next the intricacies
of the Ottoman Empire, or the industrial initiatives
of the Whig aristocracy, or Carthage, or Alexander

10

the Great, or electioneering in Halifax (a seat once occupied by his son Maurice). His conversation is replete with surprises and curious information.

His after-dinner speeches (when he can be persuaded – or tempted – to make them nowadays) are very similar to his conversation: informal yet mannered, stylized, a beguiling combination of the colloquial and the classic, often discursive, invariably apt. Inimitable is an over-used word, but not in reference to the Macmillan flavour.

During his premiership, I used to sit with him sometimes at Admiralty House, where he had been obliged to take up quarters while No. 10 was undergoing repair. These were the earliest of our innumerable private encounters, in this place or that, and I usually saw him alone, first to discuss some piece of political business for which I required approval or advice (I was then head of the party's information and publicity services). Whatever our immediate business, he lost no time in disposing of it before turning, over a glass or two of whisky, to wider discourse. One never knew what to expect. Conversations with him were indeed in the nature of a surprise packet. They were unfailingly informative, enlivening, relaxed. One always looked forward to them in the confident anticipation of learning a thing or two while at the same time enjoying his wit and geniality, and then looked back on them with pleasure. I remember many of them to this day.

He once asked me (this was in January 1962, as we sat together in the saloon at Admiralty House) if I knew how Disraeli became leader of the Tory Party. 'I'll tell you', he said.

11

It's a remarkable story. It was told to me by the late Duke of Portland, and I went away and wrote it all down. It began with his father. Shortly before Disraeli became leader of the party, the old Duke's sons, Lord George Bentinck and Lord Henry Bentinck, came to him and said: 'Father, there is only one man who can lead the Tory Party – and he is a fancy little Jew.' 'But is he a country gentleman?' asked the Duke. 'No,' they said, 'he is a fancy little Jew.' 'Only a country gentleman can lead the Tory Party,' said the Duke. 'We'll make him one,' said the sons.

Straight away they bought Hughendon for Disraeli – the Bentinck family bought Hughendon for Disraeli. But they didn't give it to him: they kept it in their own ownership for eighteen years, and then the Lord Rothschild of the day got the deeds and presented them to the Earl of Beaconsfield [as Disraeli had become].

Then a remarkable thing happened towards the end of Disraeli's life. There was another duke by now – the one who told me the story. He was twenty-three, and he had only just succeeded. He had been a young officer in the Blues, on £500 a year, and now he had come into all the vast Portland estates. He was inexperienced in public affairs and politics, and was quite unnerved one day when Disraeli's private secretary sent for him and said that Disraeli wanted to see him at Hughendon.

To his horror he discovered that he was the only guest. He was asked to put on a white tie for dinner (he was to stay the night). When he came down to dinner, there were just the three of them, Disraeli, the private secretary, and himself.

Disraeli said good evening to him, and not a single word was spoken by anyone throughout that long Victorian dinner, not one single word. Disraeli sat there impassive, glittering with all his orders, wearing the lot – the Star of India and all the rest. His face was white, and tight like a drum; he was an old, old man.

Then at the end of dinner he spoke, and he said: 'My lord duke, I have asked you here tonight because I belong to a race that never forgives an insult and never forgets a benefit. Everything I have I owe to the house of Bentinck. I thank you.'

I call that vintage Macmillan: and afterwards, that same evening, in a characteristic transfer of thought, he suddenly returned to the immediate present – to Aneurin Bevan, of whom he spoke warmly, describing him as 'my friend for many years'. He admired Bevan as a parliamentarian and liked him as an individual.

I recall another occasion, during the same winter, when I was present with John Wyndham, his devoted friend and honorary private secretary, and John Grist of the BBC, whose professional judgement as a television producer he greatly respected. We had been discussing the arrangements for a forthcoming broadcast. Business despatched, with customary expedition, we settled down to drinks in the Cabinet Room while he soliloquized on the subject of power.

The whole balance of power has changed in the world: you either belong to the Eastern bloc

13

or you belong to the other. Lots of people don't realize the change in the reality of power, but there it is, and this is the fundamental and all-important thing. Of course Elizabeth (the first Elizabeth) might have made a compact with Russia: you could say a lot for that in terms of the reality of power. But ideologically we can't do that: so we have to do the other. The United States is simply an extension of Europe, so that all the Western world, as we know it, is really one in relation to Russia and the Eastern bloc.

With that, he turned to the six States then comprising the European Economic Community, differentiating between what he termed the federalists and the nationalists, France being paramount among the latter. The federalists, as he put it, were those without a true national history – Belgium, Italy and Germany: 'The Belgians haven't got a national history. Neither have the Italians – they're Romans or they're Tuscans or whatnot. The Germans haven't really got a national history: of course parts of Germany have, but not all Germany.' Whereupon, he turned to other topics.

Lord Snowdon's appointment to the *Sunday Times*, as a photographer, had caught his attention that day, and seemed to amuse him. Not that he was in the least condescending: it was rather (I thought) that the old Edwardian found this an unlikely occupation for a brother-in-law of the Queen. He turned to the state of the Press:

The most important and the most dangerous thing in publishing is the high cost of printing. Printing wage rates have been forced up by the richest of the newspaper proprietors as the most

14

effective way of damaging their competitors. Who do you think pays the highest wage in London? It's the *Financial Times*. They pay their compositors £60 a week. [Seventeen years later, one could multiply that figure by five and still underestimate the pay of some Fleet Street compositors.]

Then he was back to larger affairs, foreseeing 'tremendous political conflict' if Britain entered the EEC:

Of course it'll split the Tory Party, and it'll split the Labour Party. Nothing like it since Peel and the Corn Laws. But it's hard to imagine the price of the people's food as a political issue nowadays: not today in the affluent society. The ha'penny loaf can't be an issue now. A tin of salmon perhaps. More likely chicken – but frozen chicken.

Conversation with him has always been the same beguiling mixture. After he had completed the sixth and final volume of his memoirs in 1973, I was sitting with him one hot afternoon in a faded old summerhouse at Birch Grove. Clad in the jacket of one suit, the trousers of another, and a well-worn cardigan, he was describing his method and manner of authorship:

I began on August 4th, 1964, just for the fun of making a few notes that day. I began seriously in January, 1965. Of course I didn't realize that it would be this length, on such a scale, but having begun you have to go on. On this scale it will be more useful to historians.

Unlike Churchill's war memoirs, his are not a work of collective or co-operative authorship. What Macmillan has published he has written himself, with graceful acknowledgments to his archivist, Miss Anne Glyn-Jones, and to his secretaries, Miss Christine Struthers and Miss Ann Macdonald, all of whom lived on the estate while the books were being prepared.

First we planned each volume in chapters, and then we made a sketch of each chapter. The main problem is that you can't tell the story like the *Annual Register*. You can't simply treat it day by day – it wouldn't make sense. You have to take episodes. We found we had to fix a terminus for each chapter, and it's quite a difficult thing to do.

When we'd worked out a chapter, Miss Glyn-Jones would produce a folder with all my papers, private letters to and from, the relevant references in my diary, the telegrams, and a chronology. As long as she could keep about three folders ahead of me we were all right.

His diaries – he wishes them to remain in the family – were no less valuable than the great haul of official papers which he has managed to amass, and are of incomparable interest. They are, as he describes them, 'little black books, like a child's book, twenty-nine or thirty volumes'. He began them during the Second World War, when he was in North Africa.

All his papers, a stupendous collection, have been moved indoors from the converted stable block in which they used to be housed, and are now properly collated. In two steel cabinets, securely locked, are the Secret files and the Very Secret files. Stacked on metal shelves, row upon row in cardboard binders, are all the other records of a lifetime – with a key or index 'in that red Prime Minister's box down there', he says, pointing to one of the grandest symbols of public office.

There was nothing hasty in the composition of the memoirs:

> I dictated to one of the girls a rough story of each chapter, without worrying about the words or the grammar. When this had been typed I very often wrote the chapter out in hand, though sometimes I re-dictated it. I tried to write as much as I could in the revises because I'm always rather frightened of dictation, for fear of becoming rhetorical. Then it was typed again. Then I corrected that draft, and it was typed yet again. Then I put it away until we came back to it at the end.

Apart from a period in 1969, when he was interrupted by a serious operation, he 'did four to five hours a day pretty well every day. I kept steadily at it, and even more steadily after my wife's death.' Lady Dorothy died suddenly in the summer of 1966. In his bereavement, the writing of the memoirs was, I believe, a considerable therapy.

Deeply interested in the political tides, trends and tendencies of the day, he is exceedingly well-disposed towards Margaret Thatcher, as he was (and is) towards her predecessor, while regretting Edward Heath's decision to go to the country over the dispute with the miners in February 1974. I

17

think, however, that he still foresees the eventual formation of a coalition – or 'national' – government. To say this is not to suggest that he is a convinced coalitionist in principle, but simply to note that he discerns a combination of interacting forces tending towards a so-called national administration.

Historically, his sympathies are unmistakably with the Whigs. To him, the Whigs were much more interesting than their Tory contemporaries. Nor does he recognize the Tories as the traditional party of wealth. As he once said to me:

> On the whole, the Tories were not magnates: they were Squire Westons – two-thousand-acre men. The magnates were the Whigs, who liked money, developed their estates, built the cotton industry, the Irish railway system, Barrow-in-Furness. They were all great magnates, and they spent their money buying pictures and things. That's what they were, the Bentincks and the rest: they were the great entrepreneurs.

Another of his interests is Oxford. He has been Chancellor of the University since 1960, when he was still Prime Minister.

> I've made Oxford a great hobby. I enjoy it very much. Fortunately, there are various colleges of which the Chancellor is Visitor – Hertford, St Edmund Hall, Pembroke and others. I so enjoy them all. Then there are the great functions in the summer. I don't interfere, of course – I'm only a sovereign in the modern sense. But people do

seek advice. I think I can be of some help to them.

I once asked him what he thought of that recent trend, the admission of women into men's colleges. 'I don't like it,' he said. 'I think it's rather hard on the women's colleges.'

He still attends the family publishing house, but no longer once a week, coming up from Birch Grove by train – at no expense to himself, incidentally, since he travels free as one of the few surviving directors of the old railway companies (his was the Great Western). His grandson, Alexander Macmillan, has told me that 'no major decision is made here without consulting him: he's so experienced – and he remembers everything.' With characteristic tenacity, and a proper appreciation of power, he retained the chairmanship of the holding company controlling the family's worldwide publishing interests until a year or two ago, when he made way for Maurice Macmillan and himself became group president.

When spending the night in London, he usually stays at the Carlton Club after a simple dinner, probably of cold meats, at Pratt's or the Beefsteak, a glass or two of whisky beforehand, a little port later on. At home in Sussex he occupies what used to be the butler's quarters in the house: a small flat – sitting room, bedroom, bathroom. Although members of his family are at hand, he has lived by himself since Lady Dorothy's death. Until very recently he was looked after by two old retainers, Mr and Mrs Stevenson.

Mrs Stevenson has died. Mr Stevenson, who still

drives him, entered his parents' service more than fifty years ago as boot boy.

The house, built by his father, has been made over to the family, but he retains the library. His love of literature is strongly marked in conversation. He has lately re-read the whole of Henry James and Turgenev: 'It's rather fun reading books you haven't read for a long time. I come back to them with great pleasure. And of course you can understand what you didn't understand when you were seventeen or eighteen.' But his sight, alas, is failing him. For someone so fond of reading, this is true hardship.

Harold Macmillan's has surely been one of the most rewarding of political retirements, if retirement is quite the word. Perhaps we should amend his phrase to read: *Non e finita la Commedia.*

Chapter 2

Macmillan became Prime Minister on 10 January 1957, a month before his sixty-third birthday. His accession was as improbable as the event from which it proceeded: Suez. He was propelled into Downing Street by the consequences of the Anglo-French 'intervention' in Egypt, one of which was the breakdown of Sir Anthony Eden's health and his ensuing resignation.

Macmillan's arrival at No. 10 may thus be ascribed to President Nasser. But for Egypt's expropriation of the Suez Canal Company in the summer of 1956, Eden's understandably angry yet intemperate reaction, and his subsequent decision to collaborate (or conspire) with France and Israel in an attempt to overthrow the Nasser régime, it seems unlikely that Macmillan could ever have hoped to attain the office, even at a later date. Eden was not robust, but had he been spared the strains of Suez, which were moral no less than physical, we may reasonably suppose that his premiership, if undistinguished, would have been prolonged beyond the point at which, in the event, he was obliged to surrender it, and that the succession thereafter would have been different.

If Eden was Nasser's victim, Macmillan was his beneficiary. Eden was put into permanent eclipse by Suez; Macmillan's political fortunes were advanced by Suez. It was a strange, even perverse, twist in national affairs that brought Macmillan to the forefront.

Britain's recovery from this ill-judged and ill-starred enterprise, and with it the recovery of the Conservative Party, was no less extraordinary. Macmillan's electoral achievements between January 1957 and the autumn of 1959, when he went to the country, are without modern precedent. Reversing the earlier prospect, he secured a parliamentary majority of a hundred, thereby sustaining his own administration for a further four years and allowing the Tories, under Sir Alec Douglas-Home, an additional year of office after his retirement. That is one measure of his political success.

Macmillan is the last of the scholar-statesmen of his generation, and at heart (as I have already suggested) may not be a Tory at all, devoted though he is to the broad Conservative interest. To some of us, and no doubt in his own estimation, he resembles more the figure of a Whig grandee – an imaginative political entrepreneur, a romantic who is nevertheless firmly anchored to the practicalities of human life and endeavour. He married into a family – the Cavendish family – of that sort. Perhaps he was already a Whig by temperament and inclination: at all events as time passed he became more and more like one. And where are the Whigs, or those of Whiggish disposition, to be found nowadays? Not in the Labour Party, seldom in the Liberal Party, but more often among the Tories.

Maurice Harold Macmillan, always called Harold, was born on 10 February 1894, the son of Maurice Crawford Macmillan and a grandson of Daniel Macmillan (1813–1857), a poor Scots boy from Arran who established the illustrious publishing house and the family fortune. 'The heroic, the dominating, figure of my childhood – all the more romantic because his life and death were so long ago – was that of my grandfather',[5] Harold Macmillan has written. Although rhetorically expressed, and exhibiting something of a rather cultivated self-image, this was evidently a lasting sentiment, never modified by the passage of time. A photograph of his grandfather's birthplace, a croft on the Cock of Arran, with an inset of Daniel, has accompanied him all his life.

If Harold Macmillan was born relatively 'grand', to become much grander still, he has always displayed pride in his family's modest beginnings, and in their intellectual interests. 'Next to that of Daniel,' he has recorded, 'the two most respected names in our household were those of Frederick Denison Maurice and Charles Kingsley.'[6] Engraved portraits of both were hanging in his father's library.

F.D. Maurice (1805–1872), now largely forgot-

23

ten, was a celebrated theologian, moralist and educationalist in his day, part founder and first principal of the Working Men's College. Under his influence, and that of the author Charles Kingsley, Daniel Macmillan joined a small but not insignificant group which later became known as the Christian Socialist Movement and was in some sense a forerunner of the Fabian Society, although more religious than political in direction. In Harold Macmillan's words, it was 'applied Christianity', representing a social impulse based upon 'an intensive feeling for the poor and the suffering'.

Harold Macmillan's father was of similar liberal outlook. He too was a person of scholarly inclination, and of rectitude, reserved, deeply respectful of Gladstone yet opposed to him over Home Rule for Ireland. His mother, beautifully portrayed by Sargent in a picture hanging at Birch Grove, was a charming and strong-willed American from Indiana, a doctor's daughter who, first married at nineteen, was widowed six months later and then came to Europe, where she met Maurice Macmillan, probably in Paris.

From Harold Macmillan's account, this was a happy home. The family's London house, sometimes crowded with members of the Women's Liberal Unionist Association, was No. 52 Cadogan Place, Belgravia. It was a tall, narrow house equipped with half a dozen servants and later a French governess. His mother spoke French as well as she spoke English, and was determined that the children should do likewise.

Arthur Balfour and his sister were frequent visitors, as were Lord Bryce, the diplomatist and historian, Lord Carlisle, who was a Howard Whig and a godfather of Harold Macmillan, and Lady Arthur

Russell, one of his godmothers. John Morley – writer, reformer and statesman – was another frequent guest. In Sussex, the family's nearest neighbour and close friend was the old High Tory Lord Robert Cecil, who later became such a champion of the League of Nations. Although shy of conspicuous political commitment, Macmillan *père* was nevertheless 'political', his wife more so.

The earliest of Harold Macmillan's 'public' memories is of Queen Victoria's Diamond Jubilee in 1897, which he recalled in a recent television broadcast of great charm:

> I remember it well. I was a child of three, but I remember it: the great procession led by Captain Ames, the tallest man in the British Army, and I saw from Mr Bain's, the bookseller's shop in the Haymarket, a great line, with British troops and troops drawn from every part of the world – Canada, Australia, New Zealand, South Africa, from India, from Ceylon, from Burma, and contingents from the different African colonies. This was the apogee, really, of the British imperial system. And, at the end of this long procession, a little hunched old lady in black to whom a quarter of the world paid fealty.

The young Harold, as he himself recounts, was a rather solitary child. His brothers were older, and there was no sister for company. Moreover he was not strong; indeed he was considered delicate, and at Summerfields, his preparatory school from the age of nine, was always sent to bed early for this reason. From Summerfields, he became a Scholar at

Eton – where in his first term he nearly died of pneumonia. He left Eton early, due to a vaguely defined heart condition, spent months at home in London as an invalid, and had a series of tutors with whom he worked for – and obtained – a Balliol Exhibition. One of the tutors was Ronald Knox, the greatest Catholic convert of his generation, who became a lifelong friend and influence – so much so that Macmillan was tempted to follow him into the Roman Church.

At Oxford, he writes in his memoirs, 'life was indeed sweet'. He was active politically, but (in his own word) confused: 'I was a Liberal-Radical, a Tory Democrat, and a Fabian Socialist.' In Union debates he usually supported the Liberal Government. Disraeli was already his hero, however. This golden interlude was short-lived, ending in 1914, just two years after it began.

Before returning to Oxford in old age, as Chancellor of the University, he had fought as an officer in the Grenadier Guards in the ghastliest of wars, served for thirty-eight years in the House of Commons, and held nine offices under the Crown, culminating in the premiership. Like all those of his generation who survived the battlefields of France, the graveyard of much of young England, he was affected for the rest of his life by the horror of their common experience, by memories of the comradeships formed in the trenches, and by an inextinguishable sense of national loss, of pride and melancholy.

He was on active service until, in September 1916, during the Battle of the Somme, he received his third wound. His earlier injuries had been relatively slight – a bullet through the right hand (which never recovered its full strength), a small but painful wound in the head, concussion. But this was critical: his left thigh was torn by machine-gun fire just below the hip. Because the wound was not drained in a French military hospital, abscesses formed and his entire body was poisoned. Thereafter he was in hospital in England, although not continuously, for two years and had to undergo a series of operations: 'I saw little of my old friends, for I was in very poor shape.' In fact he came close to death and was not finally healed until 1920.

The Battle of the Somme, perhaps the most frightful of all land battles, had opened with 57,000 British casualties – 19,000 killed – on the first day. Before it was over, five months later, Britain had lost 420,000 men: three for every two Germans. Destined to live when so many died, Macmillan was to remember the fallen ever afterwards with an enduring sadness characteristic of the best of his generation. He also remembered – with enduring contempt – those 'gentlemen in England now abed' who failed to serve, and the hard-faced war profiteers.

In 1920, when he was twenty-six, Captain Harold Macmillan married Lady Dorothy Cavendish, whom he had met while acting for a year or so as ADC to her father, the ninth Duke of Devonshire, then Governor-General of Canada. The wedding was at St Margaret's, Westminster: 'very grand, you know, with all those dukes and duchesses and marquesses on Dorothy's side', as the groom recalled to me many years later; adding, after a pause: 'but we had half a dozen OMs on our side of the church.' The OMs were Macmillan authors, among them Thomas Hardy. As a family, the Macmillans have always taken pride in their authors – very properly, one might think, considering the lustre attaching to many of them.

This was the sphere to which Harold Macmillan now applied himself, 'learning a new profession in the publishing business' and becoming, in the course of time, one of its shrewdest practitioners. But the call of politics was stronger, and in 1924, at the age of thirty, he was returned as the Conservative (or, more precisely, Unionist) member for Stockton-on-Tees.

He represented that north-eastern constituency until 1945, except for a break of two years between 1929 and 1931. Together, he and Lady Dorothy formed bonds of lasting affection with his overwhelmingly working-class constituents, and among the older generation are remembered warmly to this day. Some still write to him every year on the anniversary of Lady Dorothy's death. Nevertheless he was unseated at Stockton in the Labour landslide of 1945, and after an interval of a few months became MP for a far different sort of division, the metropolitan dormitory of Bromley in Kent, where he remained until his retirement from Parliament in 1964.

Although he attained prominence after entering the House, Macmillan was to remain a private member, a backbencher, until Churchill gave him office in the Second World War. During the intervening years the instincts previously apparent in his character, those of a radical, libertarian romantic, marked him out as one of the more interesting and impressive of the younger Conservatives.

Although those instincts were not to find their fullest practical expression or application until much later, they were already pronounced in his approach to foreign policy and to the great social issues of the period, not least unemployment. In Stockton he was witness to what he has lately called (in a broadcast this year) 'the shattering human indignity of working men in those times . . . Half my constituency, I would suppose, would be men walking up and down vaguely through the area looking for a job that everybody knew wasn't there.'

With Oliver Stanley, Robert Boothby and other 'young progressives' (decried by some of the narrower Tories as the 'YMCA') he was notably sympathetic to the trade unions and inclined towards co-partnership, while arguing that the State should assume a larger role in the regeneration and rationalization of industry. In this he displayed what was to prove a consistently liberal, yet interventionist, bias.

In the inter-related and inextricable spheres of defence and foreign affairs he was firmly aligned with Churchill and his little band of Conservative supporters in the House of Commons, among them Duff Cooper and Duncan Sandys (who became Churchill's son-in-law). All were moved by the same forebodings as the Dictators gained ground in Europe. They were united in opposition both to Hitler (Mussolini was a minor threat in contrast) and to the policy of appeasement pursued by the Conservative Prime Minister, from whose Government Eden resigned as Foreign Secretary in February 1938 because he could no longer accept

Chamberlain's attitude or his manner of diplomacy.

Thus in October 1938, a month after Chamberlain and Hitler had signed the Munich Agreement (a compact intended, in Chamberlain's phrase, to secure 'peace with honour'), Macmillan went down to Oxford to take part in the most famous by-election of the time. The Conservative candidate, Quintin Hogg (subsequently Lord Hailsham), was standing as a champion of Chamberlain and Munich. His opponent was a member of the Labour Party presenting himself as a representative of the anti-Fascist Popular Front – the celebrated A.D. Lindsay, Master of Balliol. Macmillan naturally spoke for Lindsay and against Hogg. The Lindsay slogan was 'A vote for Hogg is a vote for Hitler.' Hitler won the day, so to speak, in the sense that Hogg was returned.

In that by-election (it was for the Oxford City – not the University – seat) the convictions of four subsequent leaders of the Conservative Party were directly ranged against those of the incumbent leader: Churchill, Eden, Macmillan and Heath all opposed the Conservative candidate. Of Lindsay's supporters, the young Edward Heath, still an undergraduate at Balliol, was among the most ardent.

Looking back on this period many years afterwards, Clement Attlee, deputy to Churchill in the wartime coalition government and subsequently the most successful of Labour Prime Ministers, declared that 'but for the war' Macmillan would have been drawn into the Labour Party and eventually become its leader. Attlee's rather startling assertion – to some it must seem fanciful, even pre-posterous – is to be found in Mr James Margach's book *The Abuse of Power*.[7] In Macmillan, Attlee appears to have discerned a 'natural progression' towards Labour, and qualities of leadership as well. As we have seen, his family background did include a touch of socialism – what in his early life was often called Christian Socialism, a term seldom heard today. Attlee too – Major Attlee – had served in the trenches during the First World War, and could recognize in Macmillan some of the effects of that shared experience. In the House of Commons he had become familiar with Macmillan's radical inclinations. Moreover a number of other contemporaries of similar upbringing – among them John Strachey, Hugh Dalton, Philip Noel-Baker – were already in the Labour Party, so that Macmillan would not necessarily have felt out of place had he joined it. Finally, he was one of the 'Churchill' Tories who were united with such Labour figures as Dalton in active resistance to Chamberlain's policy of appeasement.

There can be no doubt that these were some of the considerations underlying Attlee's estimate of Macmillan's likely course. Macmillan's own tendencies were bound to commend him to social democrats of similar sentiment in the Labour Party, since they had a mutual interest in dislodging Chamberlain.

Up to the final doom-laden months before the outbreak of war, Macmillan remained in touch with prominent members of the Labour Opposition. Dalton was his principal confidant, the Etonian go-between, the main link with Attlee, the leader, and with Herbert Morrison and Stafford Cripps. Macmillan spoke frequently to Dalton,

31

who duly reported to his Labour colleagues. But the larger transactions that both had in mind did not occur. Nor did the larger meetings – meetings between Churchill, Eden, Macmillan and perhaps Duff Cooper on the one side, Attlee, Morrison, Cripps and Dalton on the other. Although projected (and Attlee was keen), they never took place for lack of agreement as to tactics and procedure among the 'Churchill' Tories. Duff Cooper would not attend without Eden, and Eden was reluctant, though Churchill was willing enough.

What they were all contemplating, but with varying degrees of resolution and commitment, was the formation of a National Government (the sort of combination that Macmillan was again advocating, although in totally different circumstances, as recently as the autumn of 1976). Macmillan's aim, as recorded by Dalton and conveyed to Attlee, was to encourage 'an influential breakaway from the Conservative Party and a union of Labour and Liberals with Tory dissentients'. On the Labour side, if Chamberlain could be brought down, Cripps for one was prepared 'to put socialism aside for the present' in the belief that 'we could agree on a programme to preserve our democratic liberties, to rebuild collective security, and for national control of our economic life'.

To Dalton, as late as October 1938, this seemed 'still very remote'. The prospect evaporated. Attlee nevertheless believed (or perhaps he persuaded himself in retrospect) that Macmillan was moving towards membership of the Labour Party. According to James Margach's account of a conversation in 1951, Attlee said: 'Approaches and talks were going on. I was in at some. I knew what was going on. I approved.'

32

Admittedly, 'talks were going on', and Attlee was 'in at some'. Their object was coalition, however (which might conceivably have been attained had the Tory dissidents shown greater cohesion and a stronger sense of purpose) – not Macmillan's admission to the Labour Party. He was ready to co-operate with Labour: war or no war, he was not ready to be converted to Labour. Attlee's was, I think, an 'idealized' conclusion in that, recognizing in Macmillan certain moral qualities similar to his own, he expected Macmillan to do what he had done many years earlier. My subject would not disagree with this interpretation.

War was declared on 3 September 1939. Macmillan now entered the first phase of a long ministerial career. He was appointed Parliamentary Secretary to the Ministry of Supply, where he found himself in an exhilarating relationship with the wayward and brilliant Lord Beaverbrook. Later, he was Parliamentary Under-Secretary of State at the Colonial Office until, in 1942, he became Minister Resident at Allied Headquarters in North-West Africa – Churchill's representative or envoy in the Mediterranean, and as such a figure of international influence. One of the numerous fruits of this exacting role was the formation of a lasting friendship with General Eisenhower.

At the age of forty-eight, Harold Macmillan was embarked, although he could hardly have guessed it, on the romantic journey that would end in Downing Street.

Chapter 3

Macmillan's first experience as a principal, as an author and executant of high policy and diplomacy, was thus acquired in the Mediterranean theatre of war. War in the self-same sphere was to convey him into the office of Prime Minister fifteen years later.

When the Eden Cabinet determined its Suez policy, ultimately committing Britain, in collusion with France and Israel, to the so-called 'intervention' in Egypt, Macmillan was Chancellor of the Exchequer. By his own admission, he shared the impulses that moved Eden from the moment when the Egyptian Government, in the person of President Nasser, seized – or nationalized – the Suez Canal Company in the summer of 1956. This was late in July.

Eden heard the news while entertaining the King of Iraq to dinner at No. 10 Downing Street. He reacted vehemently. International law and other considerations aside, not least the technical operation of the waterway without expert European management, the Canal Company belonged in good part to Britain, Disraeli having acquired the Khedive's interest for the Crown in 1875. To express it mildly, Eden was already mistrustful of Nasser. Now he was incensed. Three months later, on 29 October, Israel attacked Egypt, an action followed next day by an Anglo-French 'ultimatum' to both sides. The following day, British planes bombed Egyptian airfields; and on 5 November Anglo-French forces assaulted Port Said. 'I shared to the fullest extent responsibility for all the decisions,' Macmillan has acknowledged in his memoirs, 'all the more because I was one of the circle of colleagues whom the Prime Minister particularly consulted.'

At home, the nation was in uproar. Eden's war policy divided the country, splitting families, upsetting friendships. The tumult cut across party allegiances. While most Conservatives were (as I would maintain) all too ready to endorse the Prime Minister's action, a minority did not; to their credit two ministers, Anthony Nutting and Edward Boyle, resigned from the government. Under Hugh Gaitskell's leadership, the Labour Party in Parliament, Zionist influence notwithstanding, was largely, indeed overwhelmingly, opposed; however, many of its supporters in the constituencies were of Eden's mind, such was the prevailing xenophobia in what proved to be Britain's last attempt to sustain a broken imperial power. As R. A. Butler later wrote in *The Art of the Possible*:[8]

These were deep-seated emotions affecting

liberal-minded people, but they coalesced only too easily with less generous sentiments; the residues of illiberal resentment at the loss of Empire, the rise of coloured nationalism, the transfer of world leadership to the United States.

Reaction abroad was no less vehement. Britain was condemned in the United States, condemned in the United Nations, condemned in Asia. In the eyes and judgement of much of the world, Britain – like France – was disgraced, while allowances could perhaps be made for Israel. Britain was accused, not unjustly, of duplicity as well as aggression, of recklessness and of gross miscalculation.

Eden was not in strong health to begin with. Nor was he entirely secure politically. He had succeeded Churchill in the spring of 1955, after a long – indeed over-long – term as crown prince. Although the Tory majority was nicely augmented in the ensuing General Election, his administration had not proved particularly successful, and by the following winter there were calls for the smack of firm government, to paraphrase a demand in the *Daily Telegraph*.

Rail and dock strikes had occurred during the summer; the balance of payments had deteriorated, and R. A. Butler, then Chancellor of the Exchequer, had introduced an unpopular Budget raising or extending both purchase and profits taxes, among other unwelcome measures. The Prime Minister was widely accused of indecision, procrastination and a lack of control. He was said to be not merely uninterested in home affairs but even ill-informed about them, and the charge was no doubt true.

These were some of the domestic circumstances to which, during the summer and autumn of 1956,

Eden chose to apply – or misapply – the smack of firm government to British foreign policy by his reactions to Nasser, whom he likened (however extravagantly) to Hitler. But Nasser, as Butler has remarked, 'was no Hitler, no incarnation of evil, no megalomaniac who had to be toppled before free men could rest easy in their beds'. Characteristically, Butler was in favour of a negotiated settlement.

In the event, the physical intervention was short-lived, ignominious and futile. Ordained by self-will in defiance of professional advice, diplomatic and military, it seemed pre-ordained to failure. Three days before Christmas the expedition was over, when the last British troops withdrew from Port Said. It may be said, and not facetiously, that the only benefit accruing to Britain was the development of the mini-car, designed by Sir Alec Issigonis in anticipation of an oil shortage.

Eden's career was also over. His resignation was announced on 10 January 1957. Painfully reduced both in health and spirits, he had travelled to Sandringham two days earlier to inform the Queen of his decision. Next day he told the Cabinet. Two of his most senior colleagues, Lord Kilmuir and Lord Salisbury, there and then consulted each member of the Cabinet, interviewing them one by one as to the succession. The choice was between Butler, the more eminent, and Macmillan. By now the former was Leader of the House and Eden's deputy, while Macmillan had become Chancellor after a short spell as Foreign Secretary. As Kilmuir subsequently wrote in his book, *Political Adventure*:[9] 'An overwhelming majority of Cabinet Ministers was in favour of Macmillan, and back-bench opinion, as reported to us, strongly endorsed this view. Party feeling in the House of Commons was running very strongly against Butler at this time.' 'Back-bench opinion' was conveyed to Lords Salisbury and Kilmuir by the Chief Whip, Edward Heath.

Salisbury so informed the Queen, who had herself taken counsel of Sir Winston Churchill – and to the same effect. Macmillan became Prime Minister that day by the wish and will of what Iain Macleod was later to call, but in respect of Macmillan's own successor, the 'magic circle'. He had been 'strong' for Suez if only at the outset, until the pound began to suffer. The same could not be said of Butler, who now paid what some were inclined to call the price of prescience or prudence.

On his appointment, as Macmillan has recalled:

> The Queen received me with the greatest kindness and consideration. Although in various posts, especially as Foreign Secretary, I had seen her not infrequently, yet this was the beginning of a quite different relationship. The Prime Minister is above all the Queen's First Minister. His supreme loyalty is to her. I could not disguise from her the gravity of the situation. Indeed I remember warning her, half in joke, half in earnest, that I could not answer for the new Government lasting more than six weeks.

That is what he felt inwardly, and with good reason. Abroad, Britain's reputation had been gravely impaired. At home, the nation was undergoing a variety of emotions, none of them comfortable: shame, resentment, rancour, indignation. There was a profound loss of confidence. Macmillan's admission to the Queen was much more than half in earnest. Four and a half months later he expressed the same reservations in a letter inviting his old (but younger) friend, John Wyndham, to return to him as private secretary:

> During the last few months I have hesitated whether I would venture to write to you about the chance of your being willing to rejoin the old firm . . . The fact is that I did not really think my administration could last more than a few weeks . . .

In the event, it lasted for six years and nine months. At the outset, the disarray and dislocation caused by Suez worked to Macmillan's advantage. Things were so bad for the Government that they could hardly become worse, short of utter disaster. The party rallied behind the new Prime Minister. With their backs to the wall, the Tories united – or at least contrived to present a semblance of unity, taking on an appearance of solidarity in the face of their opponents at home and their critics abroad.

Macmillan's immediate task was to mend fences. The incoming Government was constructed with this overriding aim in mind. He had first to assure himself of Butler's support and co-operation. Macmillan wrote in retirement:

> I could imagine only too well his feelings. I realized that there would be plenty of gossips and ill-wishers who would try to make trouble between us. I knew that everything depended on our working closely together . . . He must there-

fore have the right to whatever post he might choose, in addition to the leadership of the House of Commons.

Butler elected to become Home Secretary, to Macmillan's great relief, although this meant dropping an old friend, Gwilym Lloyd George. Selwyn Lloyd was confirmed at the Foreign Office (apparently to his surprise); Peter Thorneycroft became Chancellor of the Exchequer.

With these key appointments settled, the Cabinet quickly took shape. Its membership was as follows: Lord Salisbury, Lord President of the Council; R. A. Butler, Home Secretary and Lord Privy Seal; Viscount Kilmuir, Lord Chancellor; Peter Thorneycroft, Chancellor of the Exchequer; Selwyn Lloyd, Foreign Secretary; Lord Home, Secretary of State for Commonwealth Relations; Alan Lennox-Boyd, Secretary of State for the Colonies; J. S. Maclay, Secretary of State for Scotland; Duncan Sandys, Minister of Defence; David Eccles, President of the Board of Trade; Derick Heathcoat Amory, Minister of Agriculture, Fisheries and Food; Iain Macleod, Minister of Labour and National Service; Henry Brooke, Minister of Housing and Local Government and Minister for Welsh Affairs; Lord Hailsham, Minister of Education; Percy Mills, Minister of Power; Harold Watkinson, Minister of Transport and Civil Aviation; Charles Hill, Chancellor of the Duchy of Lancaster.

Lloyd was thus one of eight who retained their previous posts, the others being Lord Salisbury, Lord Kilmuir, Lord Home, Lennox-Boyd, Heathcoat Amory, Macleod and Watkinson (who had not been a member of the Eden Cabinet). Besides Major Lloyd George, five departed: Sir Walter

Monckton, James Stuart (a brother-in-law of the Prime Minister), Antony Head, Patrick Buchan-Hepburn and Lord Selkirk, who remained in the Government as First Lord of the Admiralty but was no longer in the Cabinet. Of the newcomers, three aroused particular interest: Lord Hailsham, Sir Percy Mills and Dr Hill, the 'Radio Doctor'.

Lord Hailsham's powers as a speaker were already established in the public mind, and were now to be harnessed to the task of recovery, not least in the chairmanship of the Conservative Party, to which he was subsequently assigned. Dr Hill, well remembered as a popular broadcaster with a compelling gift for 'homely' and genial exposition, became overlord of the government information services. As he later expressed it in his book, *Both Sides of the Hill*:[10]

> I was washed into the Cabinet by the turbulent waters of Suez. The enterprise had failed; everybody was smarting under the sting of defeat and, naturally enough, the search for scapegoats was on. Those who disagreed with the Suez policy did not have to look very far for their target. Anthony Eden was their man and they chased him bitterly. But those who had supported or tolerated the venture, including Cabinet Ministers who shared the responsibility for it with Eden, did not take long to find another scapegoat in the information services ... because they were blamed I was taken into the Cabinet and told to 'co-ordinate' them.

Sir Percy Mills, a Birmingham industrialist scarcely known to the public at large, was an old friend of Macmillan and had served him well as an honorary adviser at the Ministry of Housing. As Minister, Macmillan fulfilled the Tory pledge to build 300,000 houses a year, and for this much credit was due to Sir Percy Mills.

Macmillan's first statement of policy as Prime Minister, made in a broadcast on 17 January, was of critical importance to the party's prospects of recovery. Distinctly buoyant or 'upbeat' in tone, it was characteristic of his spirit in conditions of adversity. He also provided a foretaste of the sentiments that were later to be released in his European policy – for it was Harold Macmillan, not Edward Heath, who initiated the processes which eventually led to British membership of the EEC. This is what he said:

> It is with a mixture of sorrow and pride that I speak to you as Prime Minister tonight. Sorrow, because my friend and leader has had to lay down his burden because of grievous illness. A man of character and courage. I am sure there is not one of you in this country who does not join with me in wishing him a speedy restoration to health . . . But apart from that it is a matter of very great pride to be called to the great office of Prime Minister.
> Every now and again since the war I have heard people say: 'Isn't Britain only a second- or third-class power now? Isn't she on the way out?' What nonsense! This is a great country and do not let us be ashamed to say so. It has a superb record of achievement of every kind. The country that produced men such as James Watt and his steam engine, the men who first mastered the

atom, the country that built the first atomic power station, has no reason to quiver before temporary difficulties. After all, in this year that has just passed we have had all-time record exports and the best savings for years. Twice in my lifetime I have heard the same old tale about our being a second-rate power, and I have lived to see the answer.

It is true that in the material sense — population, the tonnage of steel made, or supplies of metals and raw materials — this island cannot match the vast resources of either the United States or of Russia. All the same, Britain is not alone. Think of the Commonwealth and all that it means.

Then there are the peoples of Europe. With these countries, with France perhaps particularly, we already have close ties. I firmly believe that it is our destiny to work more and more closely with them. The total of the strength and the wealth in all these communities, Commonwealth and Europe, is no less than that of the two giant powers. But of course it is not just material resources that make a nation great. It is character and leadership, not only in government but in industry, in the trade unions, in the home, everywhere.

There are certainly some problems ahead of us. We are all pretty conscious of what they are. The shortage of petrol and oil, for instance. I do not intend tonight to go into all the pros and cons of recent events in the Middle East. I believe history will justify what we did. The difficulties we are up against are the price of paying for action. But remember the price of inaction, the price we would have had to pay for letting things slide. That might have been very high indeed.

When we think of the future of our country – and it is the future I want to talk about tonight – there is a lot to be thankful for. When I first went into politics as a very young man as the Member for Stockton, all Tees-side was suffering from the great depression that followed the First World War. The older ones among you will remember those years. I have never forgotten them. Like so many other young men I was struck with the inequalities of wealth, and especially the poverty caused by large-scale unemployment, and I rather rebelled against it. But a lot has been done since then. The great inequalities of wealth have disappeared. There is poverty and suffering still, particularly among retired folk and others with fixed incomes. But, broadly speaking, the standard of living, the level of employment and the enjoyment of life have steadily risen. We have built our defences against want and sickness, and we are proud of it. Of course, however well it is managed, it costs and must cost a great deal of money. Then there is defence. That costs money too. How are we going to pay for it all? There is only one way. By our work, our skill, our brains, our know-how – in a word, our character.

Now I must frankly come to the point on which people do differ. There is the old picture of the cake, which is our national wealth. I am sorry to drag in this old friend, but it does help to illustrate the point. There are some who are most anxious to see that the cake should be cut into slices of absolutely equal size, however thin. They are thinking of the so-called 'Equality State'. But I do not believe that is what our people want. No one should be allowed to sink

44

below a decent level but everyone should be free to rise according to his gifts, his work and his worth. There is nothing to be ashamed of in getting to the top, whether it is in your department, your profession, your business, your trade or whatever, or being paid in proportion to the size of the job you do.

The success of a country is the success of the men and women who make it up. This is the kind of thought behind the things we are going to try to do. Let me give you three examples, although you will not expect me here to announce a new policy; the place for that is Parliament.

First, power: the old sources of power – coal, gas, oil and electricity – and the new sources as well. We lead the world in the production of atomic energy for peaceful and industrial purposes, and we are going to stay in the lead. That is why I appointed as Minister of Power – not Fuel and Power – Sir Percy Mills. He has tremendous experience of business and also of working for the Government in the war and after the war – in fact he was my right-hand man in reaching the target of 300,000 houses, and I believe we went beyond it. His job is to take over the direction of all our power resources. Mind you, atomic energy is not going to solve all our problems, at least for a long time. It is not the atom yet, it is coal, and the men who get it from the ground, on whom our future will depend for many years to come. And, of course, oil. But power from all its sources is the key to the future.

Now a word on defence. We certainly cannot do without our defences. We have obligations to ourselves and to our partners. We must carry our fair share. We are going to make sure that we are not spending money on things we do not need or commitments we cannot sustain. There must be no waste of money. No vested interests, however strong, and no traditions, however good, must stand in our way.

Then there is education. It is in the schools and universities where our characters are shaped. It is there, too, that we must look for the scientists, the technologists and the techniques we shall need in such growing numbers; and that is why we are building so many new schools and why we are making it possible for more boys and girls every year to go on to the universities. That is why we are expanding our technical colleges.

There is one more thing to which I want to make reference. A lot of people are worried about our relations with the United States. The life of the free world depends upon the partner-ship between us. Any partners are bound to have their differences, now and then. I have always found it so. But true partnership is based upon respect. We do not intend to part from the Americans and we do not intend to be satellites. I am sure they would not want us to be so. The stronger we are, the better partners we shall be; and I feel certain that, as the months pass, we shall draw continually closer together with mutual confidence and respect.

I have a fine body of colleagues – that is why I chose them – to get on with the government job. That is why there is not going to be an election. I am grateful to the old colleagues who stay with me, particularly to Mr Butler, my chief partner in this new enterprise. I am grateful to the old col-leagues who thought it right to make way for others, and to those who care about what they

46

do, not what they are called; and I am bringing in some new men. I have a strong and united team. I am not bothered by this business of calculating whether we are on the left or the right of the Conservative Party. We all believe in progressive Conservatism, and we are going forward together with confidence.

Just one word more. The country expects leadership, and I shall do my best to give it. As for courage and character, I know the British people have this in full measure. All we need is confidence in our country and in ourselves. So do not let us have any more defeatist talk of second-class powers and of dreadful things to come. Britain has been great, is great and will stay great, provided we close our ranks and get on with the job.

It is not too much to say that Macmillan was deeply attached to General Eisenhower, with whom he had formed such a happy association during the war. He held him in great affection and respect. The President lost no time in writing to him:

Dear Harold — I send my warmest congratulations to you on becoming Prime Minister of the United Kingdom. Your distinguished career is well known on this side of the Atlantic, and has earned our widespread respect. My own warm admiration stems, as you know, from our association in North Africa and through the succeeding years. For me that association has been as agreeable as it has been productive.

I feel confident you will bring to your new task the same vision, determination, and sympathetic

47

understanding you have shown in the past. For myself, and for the people of the United States, let me wish you every success in carrying out the great responsibilities which now devolve upon you as Prime Minister.
With warm regards,
Sincerely,
Dwight D. Eisenhower.

To this the Prime Minister replied:

My Dear Friend – Thank you for your kind message. I too have warm and vivid memories of the time when we worked together in North Africa, and of our association since then. You know how much importance I attach to the friendship between the peoples of Britain and the United States, not least because of my own personal links with your country. I look forward to working with you once again to further this friendship.
With all good wishes,
Harold Macmillan.

But those were official exchanges. Eisenhower also wrote to him privately:

Dear Harold,
    This morning, upon learning of your designation by Her Majesty as the new Prime Minister, I sent you a formal message of congratulations, the kind that is approved even by State Departments.
    The purpose of this note is to welcome you to your new headaches. Of course you have had your share in the past, but I assure you that the

new ones will be to the old like a broken leg is to a scratched finger. The only real fun you will have is to see just how far you can keep on going with everybody chopping at you with every conceivable kind of weapon.

Knowing you so long and well I predict that your journey will be a great one. But you must remember the old adage, 'Now abideth faith, hope and charity – and greater than these is a sense of humour'.
With warm regards,
As ever,
D.E.

The US Secretary of State, John Foster Dulles, who – like the President – had been much offended by Britain's actions over Suez, sent his own good wishes to his counterpart in London, Selwyn Lloyd. These were gestures calculated to encourage the Prime Minister's conviction that the Anglo-American relationship, the partnership which he was so anxious to repair, had not been damaged irretrievably. Fortified by his own strong sentiments (and it should not be forgotten that his mother was an American) and his personal bonds with the President, he found grounds for optimism. In the event, they were not misplaced.

Chapter 4

It is natural to consider Macmillan's record in terms of those objectives to which he directed the closest personal attention, the areas of policy most strongly stamped with his own individual hall-mark, and similarly to remember the events and influences that were to strike at him directly – that is to say, at the Prime Minister himself rather than the larger administration. Because Macmillan appeared to dominate his government as 'Super-mac', he was at correspondingly heavy personal risk whenever anything went wrong: it was not so much the government as Macmillan himself who then attracted blame and censure. This was part of the price of being something more than *primus inter pares*.

At home, from first to last, and unlike his Conservative predecessors, Churchill and Eden, he was deeply occupied with the economy and its technical management. By nature an expansionist, he was anxious to stimulate the economy by liberating it, and thereby – his constant social purpose – to liberate and enlarge the lives of a nation still held back by numerous constraints, some of them the residual constraints inherent in the sacrifices of the Second World War, others deriving from six years of Labour government immediately afterwards. Disraeli's words, the 'improvement in the well-being of the people', can be said to express Macmillan's paramount domestic aim, however much, from a strict monetarist standpoint, his attempts to achieve it may have been compromised by his innate bias towards Keynesian methods. His outlook reflected Disraeli and One Nation just as it reflected Lord Randolph Churchill and Tory Democracy.

Abroad, besides recognizing the immediate need for reconciliation in the Middle East, he applied his mind to four overriding objectives. The first was to repair the damage to Anglo-American relations resulting from Suez, and to secure them firmly, as in the past. The others were: to further a policy of liberation (or 'independence') in Africa; to enter into close association with the developing European Community; and to seek a fuller measure of understanding with the Soviet Union. These were his great goals; goals to be achieved (or at least attempted) alongside the revival of a dispirited country and a Party gravely discredited. Together, they would surely have daunted a lesser spirit.

What is more, Macmillan had to accommodate himself to a new and potent influence in public life:

51

television. This he did with acknowledged success after a period of trial and error. With Mr Norman Collins as an early, sympathetic, discreet and sensitive tutor, he became a most engaging broadcaster, illustrating afresh his proficiency as 'the old entertainer'. In his broadcasts, statesman and actor were combined, as they were – but usually in more rhetorical, less 'intimate', form – in the traditional forum of the public hall or in the House of Commons.

Intellectually and otherwise, he was well equipped for the premiership. His long experience of public affairs was allied to a reflective, scholarly, good-natured and humane disposition. Moreover he was in physical shape for what is the most exacting role known to public life in Britain. Ailing childhood and severe war injuries notwithstanding, at sixty-two he was in good trim. Although not abstemious – he enjoyed champagne, whisky, port – he had seldom drunk to excess and during Lent he did not drink at all. He smoked a pipe. He ate lightly – too lightly for the family's old cook, Mrs Bell, who understandably regretted his addiction to cold meats.

In Britain, a Prime Minister's duties are continuous, never-ending. Macmillan was sustained by a sounder constitution than might have been foreseen when he was young, by Lady Dorothy, and by a private office of quite outstanding quality. Of course, all Prime Ministers have good private offices; they are never bad – but some are better than others. Macmillan's was exceptionally proficient, not only in membership or composition, but in its relationship with the many departments of state and with the party organization.

This was not by chance. He was acutely conscious of the value of a high-grade private office fortified by a party hierarchy of distinction and authority. On the party side, it should be remembered that the Conservative Central Office is the political office of the leader of the party, not of the mass membership represented by the National Union. The principal appointments were in his gift, and he made them with characteristic insight and sense of occasion: witness the calibre and personal prestige of some of his chairmen – Hailsham, Butler, Macleod and, as it were on a more 'practical', less 'philosophical' level, Oliver Poole, in organizational respects the most resourceful of them all. He was, moreover, on excellent personal terms with some of the party's most valuable outside supporters, notably Lord Renwick, whose free-enterprise organization, British United Industrialists, was a hefty contributor to Conservative funds.

Macmillan had a complement of four private secretaries at any one time, of whom Frederick Bishop, Timothy Bligh, Philip de Zulueta, Neil Cairncross, Anthony Phelps and Philip Woodfield are perhaps the best remembered after John Wyndham. Unlike Wyndham, the others were professional public servants. Freddie Bishop had been in the Cabinet Office. Philip de Zulueta was drawn from the Foreign Service. All were 'fliers' who subsequently attained importance in other spheres, although Sir Timothy Bligh, alas, died tragically early, aged fifty.

John Wyndham differed from the rest in that he

was a personal friend of long standing who had served Macmillan as an honorary private secretary for many years. They had numerous interests in common, not least a love of literature. He was very rich, a territorial grandee destined to inherit the Petworth estate in Sussex and an even larger one in Cumberland. As Lord Egremont (and Lord Leconfield), John Wyndham was also to die all too early, at the age of fifty-two.

In their years together at No. 10, the staff of the private office might truly have been called 'the good companions'. In their various and successive combinations they were a happy band, devoted to Macmillan and his interests, rather informal yet unfailingly 'correct', sometimes ruthless, usually resourceful. The companionship included Harold Evans, the Prime Minister's press secretary (or Public Relations Adviser, as he was officially known), who had been a journalist before joining the information services during the war. Moreover, it encompassed the 'Garden Rooms' (so named because they adjoined the garden of No. 10), where a corps of ladies maintained a twenty-four-hour typing service of exemplary quality. Upwards, it extended to the Secretary of the Cabinet, Sir Norman Brook, with whom Macmillan developed a most congenial partnership.

The Prime Minister had a motto, written in his own hand, which he put up in the private office and in the Cabinet Room: 'Quiet, calm deliberation disentangles every knot.' He himself observed the precept faithfully, for he was by nature inclined to quiet deliberation, although seldom as calm as outward appearance might suggest; but he could hardly claim that every knot was disentangled in the process. This was a characteristic flourish, at once admonitory, encouraging, optimistic, even self-indulgent.

Neat and orderly in his own arrangements (never misplacing a book in his library at Birch Grove), he established certain principles and methods from the outset. By definition, a Prime Minister's business is voluminous and diverse: the nation's affairs, the greater and the smaller, the more important and the less important, pass before his eyes every day. As John Wyndham later recorded, Macmillan 'made it a rule that the work which flowed in during the course of the day had to be dealt with by his private secretaries during that day unless there was a good reason for delay'.

Macmillan slept well, but not over-long. However late to bed, he tended to wake up early. He then set about his 'box', the handsome case, covered in red leather, containing the innumerable papers – minutes, submissions, letters, drafts – assembled, collected or prepared for him by the private office the previous day and placed in his bedroom last thing at night. When the secretaries arrived in the morning the box was back in their office, with the Prime Minister's comments, usually laconic, appended to each one of its multifarious contents. His observations were invariably brief: 'Tell him No. – H.M.' He was never given to wordy annotation.

One device by which his private staff kept themselves informed was called the Dip. The Dip was the repository of copies of all letters and minutes written the previous day. By dipping into it, everyone could see what the others had been up to and remain *au fait* with the Prime Minister's business.

John Wyndham was also responsible for maintaining a Bits and Pieces box, to which the staff contributed jokes or ideas for speeches or good passages left unreported from previous speeches. Churchill had kept a similar box.

Macmillan liked No. 10 as a place of residence, but it was in need of structural repair, and midway through his premiership – in the summer of 1960 – he was obliged, to his regret, to move to the grander, more formal Admiralty House, where he remained for three years, almost until his retirement. One of the charms of No. 10, as he remarked in his memoirs, 'lies in the number of small rooms which give a sense of intimacy'. Much of his contentment there he attributed to Lady Dorothy, who filled the house with children – grandchildren and others – and all their paraphernalia, and with flowers: 'But above all she made it seem like a family gathering in a country house with guests continually coming and going, with a large number of children's parties and with a sense of friendliness among all the staff and servants.'

His appreciation of Lady Dorothy in the manifold duties expected of a Prime Minister's wife, his sense of obligation to her, is indeed profound:

Even the troublesome things like formal entertaining she somehow made agreeable. She carried out all these duties with a combination of dignity and simplicity which is difficult to describe but which many will still remember. Perhaps the clue to her success was that she treated everybody exactly the same; whatever their rank or station, they were all to be regarded as friends.

Everyone who knew or met her in Downing Street or at Admiralty House will recognize the truth of that affectionate observation.

Chapter 5

In Macmillan's economic and financial policies we can discern a number of distinct and persistent strands: an attempt to modernize industry by encouraging capital investment while simultaneously expanding public services; a desire to liberate both the individual and the corporation from the enervating, dispiriting effects of excessive taxation while nevertheless extending the powers of the State; and a determination to raise the general standard of living not only appreciably but rapidly. Those were his principal aims – but we may ask whether the attendant increase in public expenditure was compatible with financial stability or was, on the contrary, conducive to inflation. To Peter Thorneycroft, it was the latter: hence his resignation as Chancellor of the Exchequer in January 1958, just a year after his appointment, along with his two Treasury ministers, Enoch Powell and

Nigel Birch.

Only a little earlier (this was in July 1957, at Bedford) Macmillan had delivered a speech containing one phrase that was to live with him ever after, indeed to haunt him, such was the notoriety subsequently attaching to five words.

Let's be frank about it.

Most of our people have *never had it so good.* Go around the country, go to the industrial towns, go to the farms, and you will see a state of prosperity such as we have never had in my lifetime — nor indeed ever in the history of this country.

To which he immediately added a note of caution, although the qualification found little place in popular memory and is seldom recalled:

What is beginning to worry some of us is 'Is it too good to be true?' or perhaps I should say 'Is it too good to last?' For amidst all this prosperity, there is one problem that has troubled us, in one way or another, ever since the war. It is the problem of rising prices. Our constant concern today is: Can prices be steadied while at the same time we maintain full employment in an expanding economy? Can we control inflation?

His warning (or admonition) was even stronger than that, however, for he went on:

The great mass of the country has for the time being been able to contract out of the effects of rising prices. But they will not be able to contract out for ever, if inflation prices us out of world

59

THE ENTERTAINER

(London Express News Service)

1 The schoolboy

2   At Oxford

3   France, September 1915

In North Africa:

4 (*Top*) With General Alexander

5 (*Bottom*) With Winston Churchill and Anthony Eden

6 Harold Macmillan announces the first £5,000 Premium Bond winner
7 Harold Macmillan and Lady Dorothy walking down the Epsom course, Derby Day 1959

8   Goodbye to Krushchev at Moscow Airport

9   Harold Macmillan and Lady Dorothy in New Delhi with the
Prime Minister, Pandit Nehru, and his daughter, Mrs Indira
Gandhi

10   With President Eisenhower at Chequers
     at Birch Grove House

11   With President Kennedy at Birch Grove House

12   Paris 1962: Lady Dorothy, President De Gaulle, Harold
        Macmillan and the French Prime Minister, M. Pompidou

13   Harold Macmillan and Hugh Gaitskell at the Sheldonian
        Theatre, Oxford, after receiving honorary degrees in Civil Law

14   Foreign contingents in the CND's Aldermaston March, 1960

15   Members of the Cabinet at Chequers: (*left to right*) Iain
Macleod, R. A. Butler, Peter Thornycroft, Harold
Macmillan, Ernest Marples, Sir Reginald Manningham-
Buller. Left, with his back to the camera, Edward Heath

16 With the Duke and Duchess of Devonshire and their shooting
party at Bolton Abbey, 1958

17 The Chancellor of the Exchequer, Peter Thornycroft, at a
Variety Club lunch

18 John Profumo, before his resignation as Secretary of State
    for War

19 Eric Lubbock and Jeremy Thorpe. Lubbock won the
    Orpington by-election for the Liberals in 1962

20, 21   Sir Alec Douglas-Home during the 1964 Election
campaign

22   R. A. Butler

23 Iain Macleod while he was Editor of the *Spectator*

24   Enoch Powell. Like Macleod, he refused to serve in Sir Alec's
Government

25 Mrs Margaret Thatcher, under heavy escort, arrives in
Downing Street, May 1979

26   Harold Macmillan, 1979, by Patrick Lichfield

markets. If that happens, we will be back in the old nightmare of unemployment. The older ones among you will know what this means. I hope the younger ones will never have to learn it. What folly to risk throwing away all that we have gained.

I gather that he appropriated the phrase 'never had it so good' from Lord Robens, who had used it in conversation with him not long before. The words and the sentiment, issuing as they did from the lips of a former Labour minister who turned from socialism, were guaranteed to appeal to Macmillan. He was, after all, the instigator of Robens's conversion, having lured him away from the Labour front-bench into the chairmanship of the National Coal Board.

In his own words, Macmillan was by nature and temperament an expansionist. Nevertheless he recognized the need for corrective action, although he believed that it could be 'relatively slight'. He 'still resisted the idea of deflation as a permanent or even prolonged policy', and in this he was egged on by his old friend Roy Harrod, who argued that the economy needed to be 'bucked up' rather than 'damped down' – a preference strongly according with Macmillan's own taste.

But in Thorneycroft he was discovering a Chancellor of markedly 'monetarist' tendency, upon whose insistence, and contrary to Macmillan's own judgement, Bank Rate was raised from five per cent to seven per cent, an unprecedented rise intended to check the heavy speculative pressure against sterling. This decision, to which Macmillan assented with considerable reluctance, was quickly followed by an even sterner stand on the part of his first Chancellor.

Thorneycroft, in the course of preparing his Budget for 1958–9, found the civil estimates too high and concluded that they must be reduced by £153 million if expenditure was to be held at the same level as in the previous year. According to Macmillan, some members of the Cabinet considered the Chancellor 'over-rigid and even pedantic'. He was certainly resolute, and – supported by Powell and Birch – would not relent. Ministers could not agree on a range of departmental economies that would meet Thorneycroft's demand, however. They shied away, for example, from changes in the social services that would increase National Insurance contributions and abolish family allowances for the second child. Deadlock resulted: and in the first week of 1958 Macmillan's fears were confirmed when Thorneycroft, Birch and Powell all resigned.

The parting was rather unpleasant. Macmillan (unwisely) described the resignation as 'a little local difficulty' and Thorneycroft's letter to him as a 'somewhat contemptuous document'. The key passages in the Chancellor's letter were these:

In the sterling crisis of last summer restrictions were placed in money terms upon the level of public investment and of Bank advances. The Government itself must in my view accept the same measure of financial discipline as it seeks to impose on others. I recognize that in order to achieve my aim some combination of politically unpopular courses would have been necessary. I nevertheless regard the limitation of government expenditure as a prerequisite to the stability of the pound, the stabilization of prices and the prestige and standing of our country in the world.

Macmillan was stung, angry rather than hurt, complaining that Thorneycroft was trying to give the impression that, alone in the Cabinet, he (the Chancellor) stood against inflation. His retort to Thorneycroft contained this rebuke:

You say that the estimates for the next year must be the exact equivalent of the sum spent this year. The rigid application of this formula, to be carried out immediately and without regard to any other consideration, would do more harm than good . . . to apply it literally must involve cuts in vital services, including those especially affecting certain aspects of family life – and this without any regard to the effect upon the industrial front and on the task of those who have the responsibility of working for wage restraint.

A few days before becoming Prime Minister, Macmillan – as Chancellor – had put forward his own central proposals in a memorandum to the Cabinet. In this he stressed the need to rebuild the reserves eroded – consumed – by Suez, and to achieve a balance of payments surplus averaging £300 million to £350 million a year. Investment, production and exports must all be stimulated, inflationary measures avoided.

It may be thought that the aim was unexceptionable; yet the ensuing policy had less effect at home, and carried less conviction abroad, than its author expected, with the result that, seven months later,

63

pressure on the pound was again increasing, there was a run on the gold reserves, and large overseas deposits were being removed from London. Because of wage increases, the national purchasing power had outstripped the rate which production could sustain, and prices were rising accordingly.

In this we can see a reflection of the old expansionist humanitarian in conflict with the cautious

6TH NOVEMBER, 1958: A NEW CHARACTER
APPEARS ON THE POLITICAL SCENE . . .

(*London Express News Service*)

and somewhat Gladstonian monetarist. But if Macmillan was at odds with his Chancellor, he was also at odds with himself: for there was an *inner* conflict too, as instinct contended with prudence and strong leanings were challenged by doubt. It is true to say, however, that his Keynesian preferences prevailed, then and thereafter. Given the natural aspirations of a democratic electorate, aspirations to which he was so keenly attuned, he could hardly have been expected to act differently; that would not have been in character.

As Thorneycroft's successor, he appointed Derick Heathcoat Amory, whose outlook was more in sympathy with his own. When he went to the country in 1959 he was able to claim that the measures of September 1957 and afterwards had proved 'outstandingly successful', in spite of Thorneycroft's forebodings. The election of 1959 was the one in which the Tories employed their most famous post-war slogan: 'Life's better with the Conservatives. Don't let Labour ruin it.' There was much to justify the assertion: material conditions had palpably improved; for many, if not most, life was unmistakably better – for the moment.

During the interim, a record surplus had been achieved in the balance of payments (this was in the first half of 1958, after the Thorneycroft resignation), gold and dollar reserves had risen to their highest level since the war, capital investment had greatly increased, as had wages and personal savings; taxation had been reduced, and there was heavy (and growing) domestic consumption. With their new spending power, large sections of the community were acquiring a sense of ease previously unknown to them – which was subsequently eroded as inflation set in.

Macmillan's immediate reward was a Conservative majority of a hundred. But, as later developments were to illustrate, that triumph did not contain the ingredients of lasting success.

During the intervening years, and with benefit of hindsight, Macmillan and his policies have been subjected to much criticism, sometimes bitter. To the writer Arianna Stassinopoulos, for example (in her book *The Other Revolution*[11]), he was scarcely less than demonic, an agent and harbinger of national decline, a materialist bent upon nothing nobler than generating a short-lived consumer boom in motor cars, washing machines, refrigerators and all the other domestic paraphernalia of a temporarily affluent society, the cynical author and proponent of the illusion 'that there is a sort of

'WELL, GENTLEMEN, I THINK WE ALL
FOUGHT A GOOD FIGHT . . .'

(*Spectator*)

Xanadu fountain that inexorably throws up riches and that this abundance is both unlimited ... and endlessly fulfilling'.

If Miss Stassinopoulos is extravagant in her strictures, and somewhat melodramatic, even lurid, she nevertheless reflects a strand of disapproval, of disillusionment and recrimination, that has gained ground in the interval.

In 1976, and expressing himself in agreeably moderate tones, Thorneycroft looked back on the rift with Macmillan. Writing in the *Spectator*, he had this to say of the year 1957:

> Like many Treasury ministers before and since, we faced some form of financial crisis. A run on the pound. An upsurge of wages and salaries. A growing rate of government expenditure. The threat of inflation. We applied certain remedies which centred on the control of the money supply. We moved the Bank rate to seven per cent, then considered a sensational step. We cut expenditure. We imposed cash limits on government departments and public authorities and told them to negotiate wage and staff levels within those limits. In plain terms we refused to finance inflation. These measures proved effective.
>
> Describing them in the House of Commons I said that the Government should not interfere with collective bargaining and that they should, where they were themselves the employer, seek to follow policies similar to those which they urged upon others.
>
> We did not therefore rely upon a wages policy,

67

though a group known as the 'three wise men' under the able chairmanship of Lord Cohen were called upon to report upon the resources likely to be available for public and private consumption, for wages and salaries, for new capital formation and other purposes. This technique fell short of the more stringent wage policies followed by later governments, but set a pattern of joint discussions of this character followed in some other countries and notably in West Germany today. The main theme was, however, a strict limit on government spending, a limitation on credit and a tough refusal to pick up the cheque for inflationary wage settlements in the public sector. The example thus set in the public sector was broadly followed in the private sector.

I used these policies that autumn as the basis of my defence of Britain's position at the meeting of the International Monetary Fund attended by central bankers and finance ministers of the free world at Washington. I said there: 'If inflationary pressure grows inside the economy, other things may alter. Other aspects of policy may have to be adjusted but the strain will not be placed upon the pound sterling.'

It is of course to be remembered that I was speaking against the background of fixed exchange rates. Nevertheless the need today [i.e. in 1976] to hold the sterling rate is no less stringent upon the Chancellor than it was in 1957 upon myself. In that year we held the rate. For a moment at least we had a reasonably firm grip of the economy. In December, however, I failed to obtain from the Prime Minister the necessary minimum degree of support for the policies which we had been following. In particular I failed to reach agreement on holding the rate of government expenditure, not at the level which had been estimated for the current year but even at the higher level actually spent. I was prepared to take our failure to contain expenditure in the current year as a basis upon which to seek success in the year ahead. I had sought to impose upon a government the same discipline as we had imposed upon the governed, and I failed. In the event, I and my colleagues left Mr Macmillan's government, explaining our reasons in what I hope can be regarded in retrospect as moderate and reasoned terms . . .

Those of us who stood then were certainly very isolated and very much alone. What is certain is that the dangers of which we warned, the perilous path which we saw opening out ahead, have been tragically fulfilled. As a nation we could have stood then at a trivial sacrifice. The price we have now to pay is a much more bitter one. What are worth considering for a moment are the factors which have impelled us on this downward course.

There was once a day – a long time ago – when the House of Commons was the guardian of the public purse. Supply for the importunate desires of kings and governments was hotly debated and often refused. Gradually this system has been eroded. The politician of the twentieth century has found himself, at least until recently, under constant pressure to demand increases rather than decreases in public expenditure. New hospitals – roads – houses – swimming pools – town halls clamoured for attention alongside a system of subventions dignified by the name of the social wage which encourages the view that an important part of a family's needs should be met by the State rather than from the pocket of the head of the household. It would of course be foolish to deride all those who have urged more spending from the public purse. In the main their motives have been of the highest. The claims for more defence, more hospitals, more social services are not to be lightly dismissed. The criticism must rather be made of governments which allowed these claims to proliferate regardless of the means available to pay for them.

We are now faced with the desperate problem of trying to cut the jungle of public spending back to size with a Civil Service of ever increasing numbers and with indexed pensions. Public expenditure has acquired a kind of vested inbuilt growth rate.

More recently (in a speech in January 1979), Enoch Powell declared:

What was heresy twenty-one years ago has long since become orthodoxy. Economists have been awarded Nobel Prizes for demonstrating what Thorneycroft was ridiculed for asserting. Everybody today knows that it is money supply that does the trick: no increase in money supply, no inflation. Everybody knows too that each domestic government is free to behave, or to refrain from behaving, in such a way as to increase the supply of that country's money.

Reflecting on the Powell speech, the *Daily Telegraph*, retracting its original judgement, agreed that Thorneycroft and his companions were right in 1958:

Mr Macmillan believed in 'big government'. With the departure of Lord Thorneycroft he was unrestrained. Inflation, so moderate throughout the mid-fifties, began to accelerate. It has been accelerating ever since. But while monetary discipline is a necessary condition for sound money, restraint in public spending is also vital if the economy is not to be ruined in the process. That is the real lesson of January 1958.

Many will no doubt concur, as they look back on subsequent events. But not Macmillan: he is not in the least disposed to assume sackcloth. He is neither defensive nor apologetic, and had this to say in a broadcast marking his eighty-fifth birthday:

> When I left office, we had a balanced budget, we had a favourable balance of trade, we had unemployment running about 600,000 to 700,000 (about two or three per cent), inflation perhaps 2·5 per cent, not more; we had a pound based on gold, we had the sterling area intact, we were bankers to half the world. We had really quite a good position.

Nevertheless, the 'little local difficulty' of 1958 did represent a watershed. He *could* have accepted the Thorneycroft prescription, he *could* have changed course, placing a check on public expenditure to immediate and continuing advantage and, by example, encouraging his successors to pursue more prudent – less expansive – policies. The moment passed. It may be said that those who followed him could have done so themselves, had they chosen. But that was not their inclination: Tory and Labour alike, they were spenders. What is more, none of them ever faced such forceful representations as were made to Macmillan. He was presented – bluntly, if not brutally – with an alternative which he preferred to dismiss: it was not in his temperament to accede to what Thorneycroft, Powell and Birch were advocating. As a consequence, public expenditure has continued to rise, with all the attendant social evils of acute inflation.

In 1957 the State spent forty per cent of the Gross National Product. The proportion grew to fifty per cent during the following ten years, and has continued to rise. With Macmillan's encouragement, his last Chancellor, Reginald Maudling, was able to stimulate a boom which did admittedly produce growth but nevertheless resulted in a balance of payments deficit approaching £800 million by 1964.

Had the country responded to Macmillan's sentiments by providing an increase in industrial productivity appropriate to the need, with all the attendant resources that this could have generated, it would not be difficult to justify his outlook. Perhaps he was too sanguine, almost too indulgent in his attitude towards his fellow countrymen, over-generous in his expectations. At all events, his hopes were not fulfilled as the years passed. As a nation, we did not advance: we declined.

It may be thought that in the broader field of domestic policy a number of measures introduced during the Macmillan era have proved similarly disappointing in their effects, although of lesser importance than a declining economy. Not that this is a comment or conclusion of peculiar application to the Macmillan Administration: no government can claim success for all its policies.

Some social innovations of the period, on occasion of a restrictive nature, have had unfortunate consequences, however. Thus a well-intentioned desire to check, if not to eradicate, soliciting in the streets has led to an increase in less open but more sinister systems of prostitution, incalculably profitable and frequently directed by Mafia-like syndicates of a dangerous order. No doubt the Street Offences Act of 1959 partially achieved one limited purpose, but its larger effect has been to extend the scope of organized crime.

Another and visible – indeed conspicuous – hallmark of the period was the addition of betting offices to our shopping thoroughfares as the old bookmakers' runners were eliminated by legislative action. With their somewhat Skid Row atmosphere and attendant derelicts, they can hardly be said to have enhanced the social complexion of our towns and cities.

On quite another plane, the abolition of National Service is more widely regretted (as I have learnt from my own observation) than might have been foreseen – but for social, not 'military', reasons. There are many who believe strongly that the values and disciplines which even a short spell in the Armed Forces might be expected to inculcate and encourage were too readily surrendered in the face of Left-wing (by definition minority) clamour.

In succeeding years, as a further consequence of Macmillan policy, the young, although not directed, were increasingly enticed into another sphere of experience, instruction and preparation for later life: higher education, from which many were ill-equipped to benefit. In accordance with the grand (or grandiose) designs of Lord Robbins and a committee appointed by the Macmillan Government, old universities were enlarged and new ones rapidly established in a massive scheme of expansion optimistically conceived as a vital instrument in the drive for industrial growth. The upshot has been what Mr Kingsley Amis (for one) foresaw when he warned: 'More will mean worse . . . Already a girl who has literally never heard of metre can come to a university to study English literature; what will her successors never have heard of if the doors are opened wider – rhyme, poem, sentence?' The resultant decline in academic standards is now universally acknowledged. An elaborate and prodigal programme has yielded no commensurate return. The streets are cluttered with ill-educated, uncultivated graduates.

But if the Government was over-active in the field of higher education, it was not active enough, one may say in retrospect, in a new and developing sphere of responsibility, that of immigration. We can now see that the incipient threat of wider racial strife and tension exemplified by the Notting Hill riots of 1959 and similar disturbances in the Midlands was not fully appreciated. A greater alertness – an acuter response – to the underlying and gathering strains might have resulted in more far-sighted policies designed to accommodate the twin responsibilities of immigration and integration, not only in Macmillan's own time as Prime Minister but under his successors. In short, it may be argued that there was a lack of provision for the future, a failure of forethought.

Chapter 6

After his resounding success in the General Election of 1959, Macmillan had been watching the swift development of the European Economic Community with close attention. The EEC and Euratom treaties had come into effect in January 1958. The first lowering of internal customs tariffs within the Community occurred a year later. Six weeks after the British election, the conventions establishing the 'rival' or 'alternative' European Free Trade Area were signed. Macmillan and his new Cabinet faced decisions of some urgency.

In the spring of 1960 a searching re-examination of European policy was put in hand by the Economic Steering Committee under the chairmanship of Sir Frank Lee, joint head of the Treasury. The committee's conclusions proved to be of the first importance in settling Macmillan's mind. He was already an established European. During the years of Tory opposition from 1945 to 1951, he had played a leading part in the European movement. He had helped to set up the Council of Europe, Churchill's brainchild. He was an enthusiastic supporter of the Schuman Plan. Back in office in 1951, however, he had seemed to lose interest, preoccupied as he was with housing, his departmental responsibility. In fact, his heart was always in the policy of European integration.

In July 1960 he reconstructed his administration. The effect was to fit the 'Europeans' in his Cabinet – mere handful though they were – into spheres of delicate importance to the development of the strategy which he was already contemplating. Christopher Soames became Minister of Agriculture and Duncan Sandys Secretary of State for Commonwealth Relations. These were spheres in which both could move with knowledge and confidence, and were of the utmost significance to the European policy as it evolved. They were spheres in which Macmillan needed ministers of such conviction about Europe that neither was likely to be compromised, or 'nobbled' – the one by the farming lobby at home, the other by the Commonwealth countries, or at least some of them.

For the Foreign Office he chose Lord Home, with Edward Heath at his side as Lord Privy Seal. Home was agreeable, Heath less so; indeed he was distinctly cool towards the proposal. He felt that after a mere nine months he had not been at the Ministry of Labour long enough to make any mark worth speaking of; more than that, he was uneasy about the projected partnership with the Foreign Secretary. He feared that as Lord Privy Seal he would find himself *under* Lord Home, a subordinate rather than an equal. No doubt he remembered how Eden had fared before the war, when, as Lord Privy Seal with responsibility for League of Nations affairs at Geneva, he was frequently at odds with his colleague the Foreign Secretary, first Sir John Simon, then Sir Samuel Hoare. Macmillan remembered this too, but was mindful of the differences as well as the similarities, and he saw Heath, in his own words, as 'principal coadjutor' to the Secretary of State, with prime responsibility for European policy. Heath was reassured after a little while, and in the event worked happily with Home.

It was in fact an apt, well-judged appointment. Heath had displayed an informed and even visionary interest in Europe since his first days in Parliament. In his maiden speech in 1950 he had commended the Schuman Plan, forerunner of the EEC, to a hostile Labour Government and a largely indifferent House. In his new role he had the advantage of knowledge and conviction.

European policy once decided, the Government gradually assembled what was probably the most accomplished team of officials ever formed in Whitehall, first to prepare the application for membership of the Community and thereafter (as things turned out) to toil night and day in the seemingly interminable negotiations that ensued. Just as there had been more than one candidate for the political – the ministerial – leadership of the delegation (both Soames and Sandys had impeccable credentials as 'Europeans' of long standing), so there was rivalry over the official appointments. Predictably enough, the grandees of the Foreign Office were pressing the claims of their own members. In particular, they proposed the Ambassador in Paris, Sir

Pierson Dixon. The Secretary of the Cabinet, Sir Norman Brook, was inclined to agree, although his colleague Sir Frank Lee (both were Joint Permanent Secretaries to the Treasury) rather favoured Eric Roll, then a Deputy Secretary at the Ministry of Agriculture. Roll had lately been running a working party on the EEC under his minister, Christopher Soames. Like Sir Frank, he was a wholehearted supporter of the policy.

Sir Norman Brook consulted Heath, but neither consulted the Prime Minister, and Sir Pierson Dixon was appointed, with Roll as his deputy. Sir Pierson was universally respected as one of the ablest members of the Foreign Service of his genera-tion. Above all, he was on very good terms with de Gaulle – respectful to that touchy spirit, yet frank and never obsequious. The President liked him, and consequently he had some influence at the Elysée Palace. This was precisely the reason for preferring him. But Sir Pierson, once he entered the Brussels negotiations, never again enjoyed quite the same influence with de Gaulle. Had he not become directly involved in them he might still have been able, as Ambassador in Paris, to maintain his old relationship with the General, perhaps to Britain's considerable advantage.

When Parliament rose for the summer recess at the end of July 1960, much remained uncertain. A year passed before Macmillan felt able to lodge the formal application for membership. During the late autumn of 1960 and the spring of 1961, in the course of a succession of exchanges between British ministers and member-governments of the Com-munity, he himself conferred with Chancellor Adenauer, President de Gaulle and the Italian Premier, Signor Fanfani. By late summer, he was ready to declare and commit himself. He announced the Government's intention to apply for membership on 31 July, nine days before submitting the application. The decision was debated and approved by both Houses of Parliament.

The year and a half that followed was a period of incessant negotiation. There were really three lots of negotiations going on at once: Heath and his colleagues negotiating in Brussels with the representatives of the six States of the EEC; Heath negotiating with individual member-governments in their own capitals; and, at home, negotiations – for that is what they amounted to – within the Cabinet and within the Conservative Party. As Macmillan had foreseen, Parliament was divided; the Labour Opposition was divided; the Tories were divided; the public was divided.

Some critics have since maintained that it was a mistake for Britain to become embroiled in economic, and especially agricultural, technicalities, because the overriding objective was to *enter* the EEC. Those who consider the negotiations ill-conducted, or at best mishandled, contend that Britain was not sufficiently advanced in her political concept of Europe. As to tactics, there is the complaint that all the important concessions made by the British delegation came too late. This argument is reinforced by the belief that General de Gaulle was probably not strong enough to impose a veto before the French elections of November 1962, after which he gained complete control of the National Assembly. It is worth noting that when in May 1962 de Gaulle delivered his first hostile statement – hostile both to Britain and to the concept of political Europe favoured by most 'Europeans' – M. Pflimlin and four MRP ministers resigned from his coalition cabinet.

Heath's speech to the EEC ministers on 10 October 1961 had established that, after prolonged introspection and self-examination, Britain had concluded that her future role lay with Europe; that what 'Europe' meant would be defined in entry negotiations (to be conducted, it was supposed, between seven separate governments and not between one government and a Community of Six); that in considering economic affairs and technicalities Britain would concede to the 'European' view rather than insist on her own as a Commonwealth and Atlantic power; and that there were terms – Britain would not join the Six at any price, but nevertheless felt reasonably sure that terms acceptable to all could be agreed. The speech represented a definite commitment, however imprecise. Heath and Macmillan no doubt regarded its imprecisions as negotiating points. Perhaps they were not yet thinking of Europe as fully shaped. They had discarded the idea of a free trade area as an alternative to the EEC, but still looked on the Community as an evolving entity that would in part be shaped by the negotiations for British entry.

What Heath said in essence was that Britain had already made a major decision – to opt for Europe – but that turning the decision into actuality would depend on the result of the negotiations. It is not easy to see that he could have done anything else. What he meant was that Britain had come to believe that she could join Europe *without damaging essential Commonwealth interests*, not that she would be prepared to join *at the expense of* at least some essential Commonwealth interests, as members of the Community supposed.

The nature of the choice was, of course, obscured or hidden by a number of political realities. There was strong domestic sentiment in favour of the Commonwealth; and party – even Cabinet – opinion, far from being fixed and settled from the outset, evolved during the negotiations. Moreover, while trying to construct an alternative to the EEC (Reginald Maudling's preference), Britain had contracted various obligations to the EFTA countries – although in practice they did not greatly affect the negotiations.

What Macmillan and Heath lacked was a free hand. Having regard to the state of British opinion, there was the possibility that terms to which they themselves might have assented would prove unacceptable to the Cabinet, the party and the country, not to speak of the Commonwealth. The Six, after all, had come together in a union because they were persuaded that events since 1914 had shown the system of relations between nation States to be ineffectual, inadequate; and as a result they had formed an attachment to an idea called Europe. Britain, on the other hand, seeking to regain lost power and influence in the world, thought of participation in the EEC not as a substitute for her Commonwealth and Anglo-American role, but as an addition to it.

It is an historical characteristic of British foreign policy to equate objective good with the British interest. Historically, it is also common to think of British foreign policy as resting on three legs – Europe, the Commonwealth and the Anglo-American alliance. This suggests that the preoccupation with the Commonwealth in 1962 was not simply sentimental or altruistic, but basic to Britain's conception of herself; and it enabled the French to exploit doubts about the British commitment to Europe.

As the long process wore on in Brussels, the British delegation discovered that every technicality of negotiation was impregnated with politics. Every single detail about food prices or textiles, however small in itself, had significance for the future political orientation of the new Europe. The direction and intention of the negotiations, and the sacrifices or concessions that Britain would make, could be expressed only in the economic terms in which the negotiations were in fact conducted.

Strategically, Macmillan was seeking a new world-role for Britain. He thought that the redirection of effort which this entailed could be formed in negotiations about economics with political and institutional implications. If his judgement was correct, the belief that he should have opted initially for a federal or supra-national Europe, and let the economics take care of themselves, is wrong. Moreover, if de Gaulle's opposition to British entry hardened during the negotiations, it would surely have emerged even earlier had Britain been espousing from the start the kind of federal Europe that he detested and was contesting with his partners.

It may therefore be said that the basic terms of discussion accepted by Macmillan – economic rather than overtly political – were right. Britain wanted an outward-looking Europe, that is a Europe whose trading and economic policies would favour the Commonwealth areas of the world. This may be considered a wise and far-sighted view of the necessary development of world trade, or as a rationalization of British self-interest, or as both.

As a result of the agricultural agreement reached by the Six in January 1962, the principle of Community preference was built into the system. This meant that all farmers in EEC countries would be treated equally in respect of each other; and second, that they would be treated better than outsiders. The arrangement could not be reconciled with the interests of either Commonwealth or British farmers.

Macmillan himself sounded the clarion when in April 1962, contrary to prime ministerial convention and moved by feelings of personal sentiment, he decided to take part in a by-election campaign. To him, this was a very special by-election, in a place always close to his heart – Stockton-on-Tees, his old constituency. Lady Dorothy accompanied him, and it was indeed a sentimental journey, marked by many expressions of affection for them both, in little notes sent to them at their hotel, in friendly greetings in the streets. There he delivered the strongest public call that he had yet made in support of the European policy:

Of course it has its risks, its pitfalls: all great transactions have. What I can now do is to hold out to you the Government's hope of success. Success in securing our Commonwealth interests. Success in securing the interests of our manufacturers and farmers. Success – at the end – in achieving an ever more dynamic influence in the affairs and the future of Western Europe and the Western world. These are high stakes – as high as any that Britain ever contemplated. High stakes – and the prospect of high reward, of peace and security, of rising prosperity and happiness for the British people: all the people, the people in the great centres of industry like Tees-side, the people in the farming belts like those nearby.

The Common Market presents us with a tremendous challenge – and a gigantic opportunity. The Government accepts that challenge. It has seized that opportunity. But, of course, we have set about our negotiations with care as well as confidence, with responsibility as well as resource. This is not child's play. This is high policy – and we know what we are doing.

That passage (there was more, in similarly ringing tones) had the intended effect: it received massive – and approving – publicity. I reproduce it for reasons that are in part perverse and self-indulgent: I wrote it myself, unprompted, because I thought that the speech already prepared, which I read in the train on the way to Stockton, was weak on Europe, not sufficiently clear-cut or decisive. Macmillan accepted the addition at once; but, having lost some of my earlier enthusiasm for Europe, I am not sure that I still agree with it.

In June, de Gaulle and Macmillan met at Château de Camps. At the time, their meeting seemed quite successful, but nothing very practical was discussed and it produced no softening of the French attitude in Brussels. Perhaps it was a mistake for Macmillan not to offer de Gaulle some concessions in the political-military field at this point.

During the summer months, Britain slowly retreated, and on Commonwealth interests began to negotiate in terms preferred by the EEC. The object was to attain through the system of the Six the same outward-looking ends as were already achieved by the Commonwealth system. But the Six refused the British pleas for 'comparable outlets'. At length, Britain agreed to give up 'comparable outlets' and discuss, instead, 'reasonable access' for Commonwealth territories and a reorganization of world trade that would ultimately rectify the imbalance between supply and need in agriculture as well as the general economic imbalance between developed and underdeveloped countries.

The Six maintained that their system, a levy on goods imported from outside the Community, was not inherently restrictive: whether it would prove so in practice depended on the price level adopted by the Community; and this, of course, was something much more than a matter of agriculture alone. They believed that, with a reasonable target price inside the EEC, the Commonwealth countries would be assured of the same revenue for a smaller quantity of exports. The Commonwealth did not like this idea, but it was fundamentally what Heath accepted on behalf of the Government. He obtained in return some guarantee that EEC prices policy would favour traditional suppliers and a certain limited promise that the EEC would take remedial action in the event of sudden damage to Commonwealth trade.

This stage was reached in August 1962. When negotiations were resumed in September, they were dominated by British agriculture. Britain proposed that there should be a twelve-year transitional period during which she would maintain her guaranteed prices and deficiency payments, but would proceed progressively to adjust to the system of the Six. Levies would gradually be imposed and British prices brought to Market levels. The cost of supporting the British farmer would gradually be shifted from the Treasury directly to the consumer. Special arrangements would be made for certain commodities.

The negotiations that followed were the toughest of all. The Six insisted that the transitional period should end on 1 January 1970, and that Britain should change to the agricultural system of the Common Market on the day of entry. This would have meant, for example, that British wheat prices would at once be raised to the lowest Market price rather than remain for the moment at their current level, which was lower than the lowest Market price. Eventually, the Six agreed to let Britain postpone price rises from the day of entry to the assembly of a new Parliament (a point of much importance to the Macmillan Government.) In essence, Britain had given way on domestic agriculture.

Heath was of course in constant communication with Macmillan and other ministers and was frequently in London for Cabinet meetings, to deliver progress reports to the Commons, or to explain himself to the Party. Party opinion had been brought round successfully, and the European policy, nicely launched at the annual conference in 1961, was overwhelmingly endorsed a year later, shortly after the publication of the Prime Minister's celebrated pamphlet *Britain, the Commonwealth and Europe.*

In retrospect, it seems that Britain was moving towards a Community which, while not perfectly to the British liking, was as agreeable as we could reasonably expect. It seems clear, too, that Britain could not have defeated France by any likely combination with the other Five. Anything that could have been done to prevent a French veto would surely have had to be done directly with General de Gaulle. Yet his meeting with de Gaulle at Château de Camps appears to have convinced Macmillan that no radical French opposition would emerge. There is reason to believe that up to then de Gaulle thought that Britain would probably withdraw from the negotiations of her own accord because the economic structure and orientation of the EEC would be unacceptable to her.

In conversation with Macmillan at Château de Camps, de Gaulle realized that he was mistaken. He then began to examine the probable political, military and economic effects of British entry, concluded that they would be undesirable, and determined to impose a veto. His objections can be summarized in the view that Britain would be an American Trojan horse.

De Gaulle appeared to differ from Britain and the US on three points: the political orientation of the EEC, whether it would have a supra-national structure or not, and whether it would be economically inward- or outward-looking. He evidently wanted an independent and perhaps neutralist Europe, while Macmillan was a firm believer in the Atlantic alliance.

On the other hand, it might have been possible to meet or at least bargain with de Gaulle if Britain had been able to make him some substantial offer, perhaps in nuclear knowledge or 'hardware'. Macmillan and Kennedy seemed to have some inkling of this later, when France was offered the Polaris submarine. However well intentioned, it was an unfortunate proposal, for at that time France could have supplied neither warheads nor launchers. De

Gaulle felt insulted.

It was commonly believed that Britain, like France, was suspicious of federal or supra-national institutions. America, on the other hand, was known to favour them. During the Brussels negotiations the Six were deliberating the future political shape of Europe among themselves. France put forward schemes which were at odds with the existing principles of supra-nationality: she wanted to concentrate power much more in the hands of individual governments. While Germany and Italy were brought round to qualified acceptance, the Benelux countries refused to fall into line unless Britain could be assured of entry.

The fact is that the British Government did not anticipate early enough either the emergence or the nature of the French opposition. The negotiations themselves, having regard to Britain's attempt not to be swallowed up in the Community but to shape it and turn it outwards, were technically well conducted. Looking back, one can see that if in the end we were taken by surprise and dismayed when the General revealed his true mind, it was because we had failed to understand him, not because we had mishandled the formal negotiations.

Things might have turned out differently if Sir Pierson Dixon had not been so heavily and directly involved in Brussels but had been allowed to lend a hand while devoting himself to his embassy in Paris. Spared the other responsibility, he would probably have been able to keep up his old relationship with de Gaulle in all its cordiality and, even if he had failed to deflect him, would surely have learned the General's mind more fully – and in good time.

The veto was of course an appalling blow to the Government. Macmillan made a television broadcast in which he maintained that the negotiations had broken down not because they were going to fail, but because they were going to succeed. The arguments advanced against Britain's membership by the French Government could have been made at the time of Britain's application, he said. The last few weeks had revealed a deep division of purpose as to the way in which the European Community should develop – as an outward-looking partnership, inspired by a spirit of inter-dependence, and determined to play a world role, not least in helping underdeveloped countries, or as a narrow and highly protectionist group, seeking a false independence without regard to the wider responsibilities and interests of the Atlantic alliance. The first conception, said Macmillan, was that of Britain and her European friends both inside and outside the Community; the second, that of the French President and Government.

Ten years were to pass before Macmillan's grand design was fulfilled and Britain entered the EEC – appropriately, under the premiership of Edward Heath. To many if not most of the British people the benefits of membership are not yet apparent, however, while a number of drawbacks – or disabilities – are all too familiar.

In 1962 (as I noted in the first chapter) Macmillan found it 'hard to imagine the price of the people's food as a political issue nowadays'. But the price of food has since become a political issue, and the increasing cost is widely attributed, in part correctly, to the policies and practices of the EEC bureaucracy in Brussels – a bureaucracy increasingly disliked in Britain. Macmillan himself now regrets – even deplores – some of the Community's more intrusive domestic proclivities and preoccupations, as he intimated in a broadcast this year: instead of 'haggling about the size of lorries', the EEC should be developing a single foreign policy, a single defence policy, a single economic policy.

As Prime Minister, he was prepared to surrender a number of United Kingdom and Commonwealth interests for the sake of securing admission to the Community. The attempt failed, only to succeed a decade later. In the result, it has proved a disappointment – or worse – to many of the original advocates, among them Macmillan himself.

Chapter 7

Macmillan had long been troubled by the dangers of a world divided between East and West; the United States and her allies on the one hand, the Soviet Union and her dependencies on the other. As Prime Minister he determined to address himself personally to an easing of the prevailing tensions. An opportunity for direct intervention – for an initiative of his own – presented itself in the autumn of 1958, with the Soviet demand, in effect an ultimatum, that the occupying powers should withdraw their forces from West Berlin, which would then become a Free City. The demand was utterly unacceptable to the Federal Republic and its allies. The governments of Britain, France and the United States were deeply disconcerted by the vehemence, not to say crudity, of the Soviet call, while Dr Adenauer, the Federal Chancellor, was profoundly alarmed.

Macmillan's mind had been increasingly occupied with thoughts of 'summitry'. He was much inclined towards an early meeting of heads of government, East and West. He had also been recalling the invitation which the Soviet leaders, Bulganin and Khrushchev, left behind when they visited the United Kingdom in 1956, during the Eden premiership. They had suggested a return visit by the British Prime Minister, date unspecified.

Macmillan now consulted Sir Patrick Reilly, the Ambassador in Moscow. Did Sir Patrick think this an opportune moment to tell the Russians that Macmillan would like to take up the invitation? After very careful consideration it was agreed that Sir Patrick should do so. The Soviet response was not immediate, and Macmillan fretted slightly, for fear of a rebuff; but in the event there was no undue delay and he learned with relief that his proposal was acceptable.

Thus, one winter day in February 1959, he embarked on what he termed a voyage of discovery – 'a reconnaisance, not a negotiation'. Although he himself had travelled privately in Russia thirty years earlier as a young MP, no head of government in the West had visited the USSR since the war.

He travelled – by Comet – with Selwyn Lloyd and a party of a dozen or so, among them the Cabinet Secretary, Sir Norman Brook, and two members of the private office at No. 10, Freddie Bishop and Philip de Zulueta, as well as Anthony Barber, his PPS, and Harold Evans, his Public Relations Adviser. For the journey, Macmillan had equipped himself with a fur coat that belonged to his late father-in-law, and a white fur hat. Thus clad, he presented a most handsome appearance as he descended from that most handsome of aeroplanes upon arrival in Moscow. Speaking for myself, I remember feeling rather proud of him – all the more so because of the contrast with his less personable Russian hosts.

I was there as the political correspondent of the London *Evening Standard*. Randolph Churchill, then the most celebrated – and certainly the most contentious – of our contributors, accompanied me. Vicky, 'Supermac's' creator, surely the greatest of modern cartoonists (and a dear friend, however much we differed politically), should have been with us, but the Soviet Embassy in London so delayed the granting of a visa that he lost patience and, before his application was conceded at the very last minute, as we were about to travel, decided – with characteristic dignity – not to go. We missed our little genius, for Vicky with his wit, charm and good nature would have enlivened still further what proved to be an unusually congenial company of English journalists, none more agreeable than the exhilarating Malcolm Muggeridge, who, on this occasion, was representing the *Daily Mirror*.

Macmillan remained in Russia from 21 February to 3 March. From Moscow he visited Kiev and then Leningrad. If his discussions – or debates – with Khrushchev were inconclusive save perhaps in two respects, they were nevertheless illuminating: and illumination was what he sought both to gain and to impart, as he intimated in his public reply to Khrushchev's speech of welcome at the airport:

> My visit has three purposes. In the first place, the Foreign Secretary and I wished to repay the

courtesy which you, Mr Prime Minister, paid to our country by your visit in 1956. We regret that the course of events has prevented an earlier return call; we are glad that a moment has now come when we can accept your hospitality.

Secondly, we hope to see something of the people, industry and agriculture of the Soviet Union. This is not my first visit; I was last here, as an ordinary tourist, some thirty years ago. I fully expect to find that conditions in the Soviet Union today are almost as different from what they were then as England today is from the picture painted by Dickens. We in Britain are glad that such great developments in your production and standard of life have taken place; and I am anxious to see them for myself. For this reason, we particularly appreciate the care which has been shown in the preparation of the programme for our visit and I am happy that we shall see the heroic city of Leningrad and the great work which has been done in reconstructing Kiev.

Thirdly, we should like our visit to contribute to a wider realization in the Soviet Union of conditions of life in Britain today and of where our country stands in the major world problems. In pursuit of this last aim, we hope to have some serious discussion with you, Mr Prime Minister, and with members of the Soviet Government. I do not come to negotiate on particular subjects. I do hope, however, that in our talks together we shall at least reach a better understanding of our points of view. Perhaps in this way our visit may help to alleviate some of the cares that at present bring anxiety to the world. That at least is my objective. Let us see if we can achieve it, together.

In private, they first discoursed on East Gemany and Berlin and the Soviet challenge to the city's existing status. Characteristically, Khrushchev was by turns rough and blustering, honeyed and appealing. As their lengthy conversations wore on, sometimes formally, sometimes informally, they proceeded to the equally contentious issues of arms limitation and control of nuclear tests, and to the feasibility, or otherwise, of an East-West 'summit' meeting.

Then, on the fourth day, Khrushchev astounded his guests, while their backs were turned, by letting fly at the Western powers in the course of a violent 'electioneering' speech. A general election (or what passes for one in Russia) was in progress at the time, and Khrushchev had been out campaigning in Moscow while the British delegation were visiting a nuclear research establishment 120 miles away. They knew nothing of his outburst until they returned – and by then the world knew too, for Tass had circulated the text. Manifestly, this was not a speech designed for home consumption, although that is what its author subsequently claimed with brazen sauciness.

Khrushchev had attacked Eisenhower, Dulles and Adenauer, and even the Shah of Persia – but in a crude attempt to divide the Allies had proposed an immediate non-aggression pact with Britain. A four-power Foreign Ministers' conference on Germany was not worthwhile, he declared. It would merely recapitulate the diplomatic Notes already exchanged and serve no useful purpose. He was prepared to negotiate a treaty of friendship with Britain for twenty-five years – or (he added facetiously) a hundred years. Such a treaty would not injure Britain's existing alliances: the USSR had no ill-will towards the friends of their friend. He favoured an extensive trade agreement with Britain. Macmillan and Lloyd were profoundly shocked by this act of provocation, which de Gaulle later characterized as outrageous.

That night Khrushchev and his leading ministers attended a reception at the British Embassy. He was in boisterous form and had (as I recall) a jolly but not very illuminating conversation with Malcolm Muggeridge, to whom he confided that he was not much amused by *Krokodil*, the Russian humorous magazine. His grandchildren made him look at it, he said, and – what was worse – explain the jokes. Malcolm sympathized and, as a former editor of *Punch*, agreed with feeling that nothing was more painful than explaining jokes. As to his outburst, Khrushchev had nothing of consequence to say, merely remarking frivolously that a good speech should consist of pepper and salt.

The rooms were noisy, hot and crowded – so much so that Macmillan became faint and had to lie down for a short while. Once recovered, he had a few minutes alone with Khrushchev: but neither said a word about the speech. The recriminations came next day, when Macmillan reproved him with measured courtesy after a good lunch and Khrushchev apologized – but only for the *length* of the speech, not its content.

The first setback – or insult – was quickly followed by another. Khrushchev had originally promised to accompany his guests to Kiev. He now discovered that he must remain in Moscow to have a tooth filled – an unlikely story, and nobody believed it. Not unnaturally, Macmillan and Lloyd felt further affronted. They were sufficiently indignant to consider breaking off the visit, and as a precaution the Comet was, I believe, ordered to stand by to fly them home. After much reflection they decided, however, to carry on with their programme, and in this were encouraged by the advice of Butler, who was presiding over the Government during the Prime Minister's absence. It was a patient, dignified and prudent decision – a decision deriving, I suggest, not only from a far-sighted appreciation of the consequences that might follow cancellation but from a generosity of spirit as well.

The affair of Khrushchev's tooth was one of several unwelcome incidents during the Macmillan excursion. Another – although not unexpected – was the 'bugging' of the very comfortable *dacha* in which he and Lloyd were housed. One of the delegation, officially described as a member of the diplomatic service, was an electronics engineer. Sure enough, he found a transmitting device in what appeared to be a flaw, or 'bubble', in the glass of some french windows. Macmillan and Lloyd thereafter trod the snowy grounds clad in galoshes, fur hats, etc., for their more delicate discussions (not that this simple precaution was guaranteed to protect them in a country replete with every scientific instrument of surveillance and espionage).

Another bizarre episode, but on a low and lighter level of importance and unmentioned in the Macmillan memoirs, was contrived by Guy Burgess, late of the British Foreign Service, who decamped to Russia in 1951 with Donald Maclean. Both were in Moscow at the time of the visit. We saw nothing of Maclean – but some of us saw Burgess. The first was Randolph Churchill. Burgess called on him at his hotel. ('I knew it was Burgess,' said Randolph, 'because he was wearing an Old Etonian tie. The only other people in Moscow entitled to wear one were myself and the Prime Minister.) A number of us met Burgess subsequently in the Ukraine Hotel, where most of the journalists were staying. I was introduced to him one night by Douglas Clark of the *Sunday Express*, with whom he had made an appointment.

What followed was an extraordinary conversation in which he asked me to pass a message to the Prime Minister. Burgess's mother, Mrs Bassett, lived in London at Arlington House, St James's. She was elderly and in failing health. He wished to pay her a visit, but feared (understandably enough) that he would not be allowed to leave England again if once he returned. He foresaw detention – arrest – unless he could secure a safe conduct. That is what he was seeking, and he asked me to convey the request to Macmillan. I agreed to do so, if only because this was a good story, and I had it to myself.

Accordingly I gave Harold Evans a note the next morning while the news (which I had already telephoned) was appearing in London. He handed it to the Cabinet Secretary, Sir Norman Brook, who duly minuted the Prime Minister. But Macmillan was too old a hand to allow himself to become directly involved in Burgess's affairs, least of all in the capital of the Soviet Union. The request was transmitted to Butler in London and of course was turned down. Butler (via Charles Hill, as I recall) intimated to the Lobby journalists at Westminster that there was nothing doing, although Burgess was never officially informed of the decision. The incident had provided a little diversion from weightier business.

In the final reckoning it may be said that Macmillan's initiative (or gamble) in embarking upon this 'voyage of discovery' accomplished two objectives of universal importance and furthered others. The Soviet ultimatum over Berlin was in effect shelved. He strengthened, if he did not actually prepare, the ground for the Nuclear Test Ban Treaty subsequently attained during his premiership. He stimulated and increased Western (as well as Soviet) support for mutual discussion and negotiation on Foreign Minister level. And he advanced – very considerably – the prospect, with all the hopes attending it, of an early East-West 'summit' meeting.

That the ensuing Summit was destroyed by the incident of the American 'spy plane', the U2, shot down over Soviet territory on 1 May 1960 while the Heads of Government were gathering in Paris, was no fault of his. The Summit was wrecked – abandoned – because Macmillan's old comrade-in-arms, President Eisenhower, had allowed his Intelligence services a degree of licence which on this occasion proved disastrous. Macmillan was deeply downcast – just as millions were outraged by America's ineptitude.

Since Stalin's death and the struggle for power that ensued, resulting in Khrushchev's succession and supremacy, Eisenhower and other Western leaders – like those of the Soviet Union – had become increasingly preoccupied with what Malenkov (first and interim premier after Stalin) bleakly called 'the modern means of destruction', the awful products of the Nuclear Age. On the part of the Soviets, traditional (or conventional) attachment to the 'inevitability' of conflict between communist and capitalist societies had given way, or almost so, to a chilling realization that both might be destroyed – simultaneously and even 'inadvertently', as it were – by the new military science. Hence the race for nuclear 'superiority' while attempting – or professing to attempt – some form of control. Hence, also, Eisenhower's recourse, after the Soviet rejection in 1955 of his 'open skies' policy, to the aerial surveillance of which Francis Gary Powers and the U2 were such ill-fated instruments. The first of these flights had been authorized in 1956. Four years later, it appears, no one thought to suspend them – and thus the Summit, in which so many were reposing so much hope, was extinguished.

Macmillan was painfully dejected when some of us saw him at the Embassy in Paris immediately afterwards. No doubt his personal disappointment was all the more intense because he knew that while he himself had acted impeccably, contributing moral purpose, political will and well-judged diplomacy to the attempt to secure a better international order, the larger influences deriving from physical power remained with the United States as the arsenal and guardian of the Western democracies. At least for the present, there was little more that he himself could do.

He may also have reflected that British military strength, and with it our political influence, could have been greater, had conviction and the state of the economy encouraged successive administrations, his own included, to pursue the more self-sufficient defence policies which British science and industry were amply capable of sustaining. But our military capacity – and consequently our political influence – had been impaired.

At the end of the Second World War, Britain was outstandingly proficient in the development of advanced weaponry, nuclear and otherwise. Our superiority, universally acknowledged, and owing much to Churchill's interest and understanding, was quickly lost, however. For example, the swing-wing fighter, among other British inventions, was given away to the Americans, on whom we became ever more dependent.

In the missile field we developed Blue Streak, a formidable ground-to-ground missile which, alas, blew up on its first launching. After this setback, the Government was quick to lose confidence in it, and Macmillan then persuaded the United States to let us have Skybolt, an American rocket descended from Blue Streak. But Skybolt also blew up, and was immediately dumped by the Pentagon.

The one major nuclear arm available to Britain since has been the Polaris submarine, equipped with American ballistic missiles. Britain is not without nuclear defence: but – except by derivation – the instruments of that defence are not the products of British science and engineering.

Personal, i.e. public, attitudes to defence had, of course, been affected from the mid-fifties to the early sixties by that most vehement and tireless of extra-Parliamentary forces, the Campaign for Nuclear Disarmament, ever-active under the inspiration of Canon John Collins and his undeniably interesting, if somewhat élitist, associates of the Left intelligentsia – Michael Foot, Vicky the

101

cartoonist, the writer James Cameron and others of scarcely less arresting qualities as superior propagandists in a popular cause. What we do not know, however, is the real effect of the CND on national will and public policy. There can be no doubt that the movement exercised a considerable influence: how much, we cannot tell.

What we do know is that it disrupted the Labour Party under the leadership of Hugh Gaitskell, whose own sound sentiments and convictions were utterly opposed to those of the disarmers and neutralists in his midst, however many they were. Hence his resounding words at the Labour Party conference of 1960, when he defied them all with his declaration that he would 'fight and fight and fight again' to preserve the principles in which he himself believed. Myself, I have never heard a more noble utterance from a political platform – not that his differences with his critics were confined to the issue of nuclear disarmament: he was also at odds with them over Clause IV of the party's constitution, that all-embracing article of faith providing for 'the common ownership of the means of production, distribution and exchange'.

Chapter 8

Macmillan once told me: 'Three parts of my time as Prime Minister were occupied with overseas affairs' – a proportion reflected in the balance of his memoirs. Some were affairs of an inherently British or Commonwealth nature, deriving from the imperial past: developments in Cyprus, Rhodesia, the Persian Gulf. Others were of a broader international character: apart from relations with Russia, the East-West contest for nuclear parity (or supremacy) and the Cuban missile crisis, they included the accelerating movement towards independence in Africa, the Chinese threat to India, and, of course, his grand design in Europe, encompassing both foreign and domestic policy. All this involved extensive travel. During the course of his premiership he visited France, Russia, Germany, Pakistan, India, Ceylon, Singapore, New Zealand, Australia, Ghana, Nigeria, Zambia, Malawi, Rhodesia, South Africa, the West Indies, Canada and the United States.

Despite the weight of his responsibilities abroad he was none the less able to give remarkably close attention to the direction of home affairs. In this, he was assisted by an accident of history, and of age, by which I mean that personal friendships are of great help in the conduct of international discussions or negotiations, not only because they are usually conducive to harmony but also because ease and familiarity reduce the wear and tear and more often than not save time.

Macmillan was fortunate in that he already knew the political leaders abroad – those in the Western world, that is – with whom he had to do business. 'For ten years after the war we had the advantage of friendships made in war,' he once remarked to me in conversation at Birch Grove. 'I knew them all.'

He went on (as I had rather expected) to speak of two in particular, Presidents Eisenhower and Kennedy, both of whom he deeply admired:

I think people now realize what a fine man Ike was. He was a sort of Duke of Wellington of America. I was lucky to have him. Suddenly after him came this young brilliant figure, John Kennedy. I had a vague recollection of him earlier because his sister had married my – no, my wife's – nephew, Billy Burlington [Lord Burlington, later the Marquess of Hartington]. This young man, a pioneer while I was an ageing Prime Minister between sixty and sixty-five, he came here to this house. I had with two Presidents this extraordinary relationship: I was a sort of son to Ike, and it was the other way round with Kennedy.

Just as his bonds with Eisenhower were cemented in war, his bonds with Kennedy were cemented under the threat of war when in October 1962 the peace of the world hung by a thread. Under Castro, Cuba was being prepared as a base for a Soviet offensive against the United States. Sites had been armed with long-range ballistic missiles directed towards the great cities of America. It soon became apparent that they represented much of Russia's available nuclear strength. On Monday, 22 October, Macmillan wrote in his diary: 'The first day of the World Crisis!' His phrase did not exaggerate the peril confronting the West – though now, only seventeen years later, the magnitude of the challenge is largely forgotten.

He had been alerted to the danger the previous night by the British Ambassador in Washington, David Ormsby Gore, whose warning was quickly followed by a 'most private' – and most solemn – message from President Kennedy, teletyped into Admiralty House. Macmillan was the first person abroad – the first of the allied leaders – to whom Kennedy turned in this extremity. Separated by the width of the Atlantic ocean, but in unbroken communication, he remained at the President's side, as it were, throughout the developing crisis, from the first day to the last, when the Soviets climbed down and agreed to dismantle their rockets.

Macmillan's influence with Kennedy in the gravest threat to world peace since the war was not understood at the time except by a few of his intimates; nor is it widely recognized even now. The President reposed in him a degree of confidence extended to no other allied statesman, and to only a handful of his compatriots in Washington.

But the public did not know this – could not know it, given the delicacy of their transactions. Indeed the British Government was depicted by the Labour opposition in the House of Commons as having no say in events, or none worth speaking of: so much for our 'special relationship' with America. British newspapers were similarly sceptical or dismissive, but with rather more excuse than the parliamentary opposition, whose leader, Hugh Gaitskell, had been taken into Macmillan's confidence, at least partially, along with Harold Wilson and George Brown. (Macmillan found Gaitskell and Wilson rather 'wet' in their response, George Brown more robust.)

In fact, the 'special relationship' had seldom been more fruitfully invoked or fulfilled. Apart from Kennedy's respect for Macmillan's judgement, and the cordiality between them, each enjoyed the advantage – it was a mutual advantage – of an admirable intermediary, an invaluable confidant, in the person of Ormsby Gore (now Lord Harlech), a personal friend of both the President and the Prime Minister.

Among other things, Macmillan advised Kennedy against the worldwide NATO 'alert' – the summons to action stations – which was being urged upon him in Washington and could have had little, if any, constructive significance. As Macmillan wisely observed: 'mobilization' had sometimes been a cause of war. (In Britain, incidentally, such an 'alert' would have involved a Royal Proclamation and the call-up of reservists.)

To study the origin and course of the Cuban missile crisis, as recapitulated at length in his memoirs, is to understand something of Macmillan's vision. His account, replete with presidential texts and other exchanges, is probably the most instructive and dramatic chapter in his sixth and final volume. His account of John Kennedy's visit to Birch Grove eight months afterwards is less important but on a personal level even more moving.

Kennedy spent a summer weekend with him in 1963, accompanied (needless to say) by much of the vast apparatus of the presidency: immense security and communications staffs, cohorts of officials of every rank and degree from ambassador to cipher clerk. US Army engineers installed four hundred telephone lines; in Brighton, the Grand and Metropole hotels were taken over. Maurice Macmillan's house on the estate at Birch Grove became the forward communications centre. But at least the family were spared some of the domestic trials of an earlier visit by de Gaulle, when Mrs Bell, the cook, had complained about having to store a supply of the General's blood plasma in her refrigerator (Kennedy had his own ambulance plane in attendance), and the head gamekeeper, Mr Blake, had been indignant because security squads were investing his woods and disturbing the pheasants.

To Macmillan, dazzled by the heroic presence of the young President (and a good part of his court), this was perhaps the most romantic episode of a long premiership. The main business of that short weekend – it was really of twenty-four hours, from Saturday to Sunday – was the prospective Test Ban Treaty, presently attained. Macmillan was greatly gratified by the President's encouragement and support for his efforts.

In his memoirs, he has described their leave-taking: 'I can see the helicopter now, sailing down the valley above the heavily laden, lush foliage of oaks and beech at the end of June. He was gone. Alas, I was never to see my friend again. Before those leaves had turned and fallen he was snatched by an assassin's bullet from the service of his own country and the whole world.'

Macmillan's own long period of office was also to end within the same short space of time. Even before the violent death of poor John Kennedy, his elderly friend, the last Edwardian remaining in public life, found himself obliged to resign.

Although Macmillan's friendship with the first of 'his' American Presidents was formed in Africa, albeit on its northern, Mediterranean shores, there is no reason to think that his response to the innumerable pressures for independence throughout that continent, a response memorably expressed in his 'wind of change' speech, was directly affected by either of them except in the sense that he was closely and continuously exposed to the settled and long reiterated American belief in the merits of colonial liberation. The famous speech was delivered to both Houses of the South African Parliament in February 1960. Contentious at the time (and offensive to his hosts), it has remained contentious: Macmillan's critics accuse him of having contributed to a weakening of white authority, to the encouragement of black nationalist demands and the abdication of European responsibilities in Africa, the surrender of Western interests, not least in Rhodesia. To others it seemed, and still seems, a speech of reason, realism and moderation.

We do not know who suggested the words 'wind

of change'. If John Wyndham, who was with him, could not discover the authorship, neither can I: nor is it worth further inquiry, for the phrase is commonplace enough, subsequent fame or notoriety notwithstanding. The key passages were these:

Ever since the break-up of the Roman Empire one of the constant facts of political life in Europe has been the emergence of independent nations. They have come into existence over the centuries in different forms, with different kinds of Government, but all have been inspired by a deep, keen feeling of nationalism, which has grown as the nations have grown.

In the twentieth century, and especially since the end of the war, the processes which gave birth to the nation States of Europe have been repeated all over the world. We have seen the awakening of national consciousness in peoples who have for centuries lived in dependence upon some other power. Fifteen years ago this movement spread through Asia. Many countries there of different races and civilizations pressed their claim to an independent national life. Today the same thing is happening in Africa, and the most striking of all the impressions I have formed since I left London a month ago is of the strength of this African national consciousness. In different places it takes different forms, but it is happening everywhere. The wind of change is blowing through this continent, and, whether we like it or not, this growth of national consciousness is a political fact. We must all accept it as a fact, and our national policies must take account of it.

Of course, you understand this better than

anyone. You are sprung from Europe, the home of nationalism, and here in Africa you have yourselves created a new nation. Indeed, in the history of our times yours will be recorded as the first of the African nationalisms, and this tide of national consciousness which is now rising in Africa is a fact for which you and we and the other nations of the Western World are ultimately responsible. For its causes are to be found in the achievements of Western civilization, in the pushing forward of the frontiers of knowledge, in the applying of science in the service of the human needs, in the expanding of food production, in the speeding and multiplying of the means of communication and, perhaps above all, the spread of education.

It is a basic principle of our modern Commonwealth that we respect each other's sovereignty in matters of internal policy. At the same time we must recognize that in this shrinking world in which we live today the internal policies of one nation may have effects outside it. We may sometimes be tempted to say to each other: 'Mind your own business'; and in these days I would myself expand the old saying, so that it runs: 'Mind your own business and mind how it affects my business too.'

As a fellow member of the Commonwealth it is our earnest desire to give South Africa our support and encouragement, but I hope you won't mind my saying frankly that there are some aspects of your policies which make it impossible for us to do this without being false to our own deep convictions about the political destinies of free men to which in our own territories we are trying to give effect.

The South African premier, Dr Verwoerd, apostle of white supremacy and apartheid, in whom Macmillan had detected a strong Calvinistic streak ('He was certainly as convinced as John Knox himself that he alone could be right'), was understandably put out, affronted. Macmillan was unrepentant, and has never regretted his candour. As John Wyndham wrote later, in his own memoirs:[12]

Mr Macmillan, in fact, said nothing which should have seemed startling or novel. He spoke about the force of African nationalism. Of course. It was something that existed throughout the whole wide continent. He spoke quietly and logically about the need to come to terms with African nationalism as a political fact . . . All this was simply a restatement of British policy. Anyone who had expected Mr Macmillan to speak otherwise must have been totally unaware of his innate courage.

En route to South Africa, while visiting Ghana, he had in fact expressed the same sentiment, employing the self-same phrase, 'wind of change', but without arousing much attention, although he did catch the acute if distant ear of Sir Roy Welensky, who – embattled (as ever) in the defence of white Rhodesia – feared the probable consequences of what Macmillan was saying and felt forewarned of the ensuing and stronger restatement.

A restatement, yes; but an emphatic one: so emphatic in its terms and implications as to set Britain upon a lasting and irreversible course in pursuit of policies more or less consistent with his own liberal (or liberating) instincts – instincts commanding wide popular support at home. European policy perhaps excepted, this was probably true of all his important overseas – or international – initiatives, most notably in relation to Russia: they were in tune with much domestic sentiment.

Over Africa, they were in accord with even wider sentiments, however. They reflected a European, and indeed a larger Western, disavowal of colonial authority and responsibility – as critics of withdrawal would say, a lack of will to sustain the imperial tradition, a failure of spirit. In Welensky's bitter phrase, they represented a tendency to 'run before the tempest', to bow and abdicate. His strictures on successive British ministers – Lennox-Boyd, Macleod (especially), Maudling, Home, Butler – may be unjust. The effect of their policies under Macmillan was nevertheless towards black rule in every British colony.

After the Belgian débâcle in the Congo, and in common with other Western statesmen, they recognized (or they believed) that the European powers had no popularly acceptable alternative to surrender in Africa – surrender on the best (or almost any) terms obtainable. Among British ministers, this instinct was no doubt heightened by the painful memories of Suez – and they were probably right. Would Kenya be more stable today, if we had tried to maintain our rule in the face of African opposition? Could other measures have perpetuated white supremacy in Rhodesia, given the strength of African nationalism? Would South Africa itself have become more settled if Macmillan had never spoken? From the point of view of the white communities in Africa, Macmillan's policy may not seem particularly noble – but it was not ignoble.

Nor was it casual or ill-considered. He followed what he believed to be the course best calculated to serve the longer-term Western (or democratic) interest. In doing so he offended many of the whites in Africa – but not all of them.

Chapter 9

The defeat of his European policy in 1962, which affected him deeply, marked the opening of Macmillan's final phase as Prime Minister. He felt the blow acutely – all the more acutely since it followed a year of trial and anxiety at home. Things were no longer the same around the Cabinet table: a number of familiar faces had disappeared. During the previous summer, after a winter and spring of mounting discontent on the domestic front, painfully dramatized in the Orpington by-election, when the Liberals overturned a Tory majority of nearly 15,000, he had removed seven Cabinet ministers at a stroke.

Selwyn Lloyd, Chancellor of the Exchequer, had been required to resign on Friday, 13 July, along with Lord Kilmuir, the Lord Chancellor, John Maclay, Secretary for Scotland, Harold Watkinson, Minister of Defence, Lord Mills, Minister without

Portfolio, Dr Charles Hill, Minister of Housing and Local Government, and Sir David Eccles, Minister of Education.

Lloyd's offence – and Selwyn Lloyd was the foremost victim – was failure to commend his 'pay pause' to the public and gain popular acceptance of what was, in retrospective comparison with more recent restraints, a measure of rather mild character. Macmillan had noted in his diary (8 July 1962):

> Selwyn seems to me to have lost grip . . . Lately, he seems hardly to function in some vital matters – e.g. this Incomes Policy affair. The Pay Pause started a year ago, exactly. By the end of the year, it was clear that it was to be succeeded by a more permanent policy. In spite of continual pressure from me, *nothing* at all was done, except long and fruitless discussions . . . the Chancellor of the Exchequer *ought* to have got going at least after the turn of the year.

That was Lloyd's alleged offence: but perhaps there was more to it, for Lloyd and his Chief Secretary, Henry Brooke (who were now replaced by Reginald Maudling and John Boyd-Carpenter), were personally identified with the Treasury's anxiety, not to say alarm, over the growing volume of public expenditure. Maudling, in contrast, was somewhat after the Prime Minister's own heart, a neo-Keynesian. Apprehensions on this account were not allayed by Macmillan's enthusiasm for the incalculably expensive Concorde programme (supersonic in more senses than one), about which the Treasury and many others had well-founded reservations.

As for the other victims of the ministerial massacre, there were no imputations of departmental or political failure. They were sacrificed for reasons of stage management, to provide a change of cast, a set of new faces.

It was a staggering decision, to which – apart from Tim Bligh and others in the Prime Minister's private office – only Butler, Macleod (then chairman of the party) and the Chief Whip, Martin Redmayne, were privy in advance. My own understanding at the time was that Iain Macleod had been particularly pressing in demanding a 'new look': he was rather given to that sort of thing. Not all the surviving ministers approved of Macmillan's action. Nor were Conservative backbenchers reassured by this display of ruthlessness. If anything, it increased the unrest in the parliamentary party. But there were other strains, too, strains of a different nature.

In the autumn of 1962, William Vassall, an Admiralty clerk in the office of the Civil Lord, Tam Galbraith, had been arrested for spying and was duly convicted. Because of imputations in the newspapers against the character of Mr Galbraith, Macmillan set up a tribunal of inquiry which, besides clearing the Civil Lord of unfounded allegations, resulted in the jailing of two journalists. The sentences were strongly resented in Fleet Street – and of course Macmillan was blamed.

Thus the Government was at a low ebb, not only in Fleet Street but in Parliament and in the country, early in 1963. In no time at all came a further shock. Before the winter was out, Westminster was again alive with rumours involving another minister, John Profumo, the Secretary of State for War.

Profumo was said to be having an affair with a girl called Christine Keeler, while the naval attaché from the Soviet Embassy was also enjoying her favours. The good-looking Miss Keeler was known, moreover, as a lady of doubtful reputation. Word reached the Prime Minister's private office from more than one quarter, including an informant in Paris.

John Wyndham was among the first to hear it – from an old friend, Mark Chapman-Walker, managing director of the *News of the World*, who had asked to see him urgently. Wyndham at once informed Bligh, the principal private secretary, and Redmayne, the Chief Whip. They consulted MI5. Yes, they were told, it was true that Profumo had been 'in and out of Miss Keeler's place', and had been warned against the association. The authorities were sure, however, that there had been no security risk.

Bligh spoke to Profumo. Taxed with the accusation, Profumo denied it. He subsequently denied it in the House of Commons – but later, under continuing pressure, admitted the truth. His resignation followed, and with it his political eclipse. Both he and the Government paid a heavy penalty.

The consequences could have been alleviated, I believe, although not entirely averted, if Macmillan himself had taken a hand at the right time. He himself ought surely to have interviewed Profumo at the outset, instead of leaving the inquiries to subordinates and simply reading the resulting minutes.

Somewhat 'pi' by nature, he shied away from that course. To my mind, it is scarcely conceivable that Profumo would have lied to his Prime Minister, face to face in the Cabinet Room, just the two of them. But for the private lie, there need never have been a public lie in the House – the occasion would not have arisen. Had Macmillan confronted him personally, he would almost certainly have learnt the truth from Profumo, whose resignation could then have been arranged immediately and the scandal thereby contained, instead of being allowed to develop such far-reaching proportions.

Far-reaching is the right term, for rumour and innuendo, scandal (real or alleged), was not confined to John Profumo but encompassed – enmeshed – other ministers. Most of it was ludicrously extravagant, preposterous, bizarre. Some was nearer the mark, however – and one story threatened the Government with destruction because it proved true and involved a minister who (unlike the more junior Profumo) was a member of the Cabinet.

This minister admitted to Macmillan one night that he had indeed been compromised, as gossip had it, by a certain erotic adventure (not, I may say, of any stunningly exotic character). Accordingly, he was proposing to resign after a meeting of the Cabinet next morning. But, having slept on his troubles, he changed his mind, judging – correctly, as it turned out – that if he stood firm and confessed nothing in public the rumours would presently lose force.

Macmillan had been emotionally prepared to announce the Government's resignation at once. He was convinced that the administration could not withstand a further blow to its moral authority. He had already confided his intention to the friend with whom, in the event, he was able to lunch more comfortably that day, reprieved as it were, and relieved by his escape, but shocked by the experience. The public knew nothing of this, however.

Over Profumo, Macmillan had received many moving expressions of public sympathy, conveyed to him in several thousands of kindly letters. The party in Parliament remained anxious, uneasy and apprehensive, however, and by the summer there were repeated reports that he would soon give up. True, he had informed the 1922 Committee that he would lead the party into the next election; but this was in April, two months before the final explosion of Profumo's resignation, which inevitably gave rise to further misgivings about his capacity to continue in office. It was increasingly said that he had lost his grip.

The reservations about him were not confined to the backbenches. Some of 'the colleagues', his fellow members of the Cabinet, were similarly critical and thought that he should go. By now they knew more about the Profumo episode, its history and its consequences than anyone else. They detected a failure of judgement on the Prime Minister's part. Moreover, they realized just how close to collapse the Government had come in the aftermath. They had all been on the edge of the precipice, and were understandably nervous.

When Parliament rose for the long summer recess, however, the general (and even the informed) impression was that Macmillan intended to stay, whatever his critics might say. During August he gave every sign of determination to carry on. For one thing, he involved himself in some of the Party's preparations for the autumn − the October conference, the opening of the new session of Parliament, and all the attendant activities that mark the beginning of the political year.

He was especially interested not only in the composition but also in the production of a party pamphlet called *Acceleration*, a statement of policy bearing his photograph and signature, which was to be issued just before the conference. Once a week throughout August he assembled Sir Michael Fraser, head of the Research Department, Peter Goldman, director of the Conservative Political Centre and myself in the Cabinet Room at Admiralty House to discuss it. No detail was too small for his consideration: he even revised the captions to some of the illustrations (this of course was the old publisher at work).

But he was not well. He had not been well for several months, though very few knew it. He was in fact contemplating retirement. By September, perhaps half a dozen people understood his intentions. He confided in his son, Maurice Macmillan, in his son-in-law, Julian Amery, in Timothy Bligh, in Lord Poole (who in April had reappeared on the political scene as joint chairman of the Party with Iain Macleod) and in Butler. Macleod, to all appearances and certainly in terms of electoral weight the senior member of the partnership then reigning over the Conservative Central Office, was neither consulted nor informed.

It was provisionally agreed in September that Macmillan should attend the party conference at Blackpool in October, travelling (as usual) on the Friday in order to speak next day, and then, at the end of an otherwise 'normal' speech, announce his decision to retire in January 1964. Later in the month, however, he himself and some of those in his confidence were having second thoughts. He was urged to say nothing of the sort at Blackpool, and to declare instead that he meant to carry on.

But suddenly another course was forced upon him. As the party conference was assembling at Blackpool on the night of Tuesday, 8 October, the news came through that illness had finally struck him down: the growth of his prostate gland was such that he must enter hospital at once for an immediate operation. Only Lord Poole (as I remember) seemed less than surprised: it appeared that he knew rather more than his colleagues, had heard something earlier, and was better prepared both for what had happened and for what was to follow.

What followed was of course the struggle for the Tory leadership – the last to be determined by what Macleod later called the 'magic circle'. Macmillan's first favourite was Lord Hailsham, whose succession had become practicable because of recent legislation enabling peers to renounce their peerages. But to many members of the Party, including some of the best and most influential, Butler, the deputy Prime Minister, seemed the right and natural, almost the lawful, heir.

Some months previously, when ministers and others were discussing the likelihood of an early change, 'Rab' had intimated that he was no longer to be considered a candidate for the premiership because he felt that he could not reunite the party. Friends of his thought differently, however, and persuaded him to change his mind. By the time of Macmillan's resignation he was again ready to accept nomination. So was Maudling; Macleod too – though he assessed his prospects as very slight and made little if any attempt to promote himself.

Nor did the eventual successor, Lord Home. On the contrary, Home was sought out, appealed to, and in effect drafted, as reservations were expressed about the suitability of both Hailsham and Butler, and as Maudling failed to make headway.

The leadership crisis divided the Party bitterly and remains a source of recrimination to this day. With each of the various factions contending for its own candidate, the ordinary business of the Blackpool conference was utterly disrupted and finally concluded in an atmosphere close to pandemonium and hysteria. As the principals returned to London, the struggle continued with gathering passion.

While still in Blackpool, officers of the party's National Union – Lord Chelmer, Dame Margaret Shepherd, Sir Theodore Constantine, Sir John Howard – had begun a series of confidential polls among constituency and area chairmen in an attempt to establish so-called 'grass roots' sentiment. I recall that these inquiries, resumed in London, produced six names in all, though at different stages: Hailsham, Home, Butler, Maudling, Macleod and Heath.

If Heath had the least support of all, he was nevertheless present in the lists, without having tried; and in the light of his own accession to the leadership less than two years later it is worth noting that he himself voted for Home in the poll of ministers conducted by the Lord Chancellor, Lord Dilhorne, at Macmillan's behest. No doubt there was an element of self-interest in his preference. If either of his contemporaries, Maudling or Macleod, had secured the succession, Heath could hardly have expected to rise above him in the future. If Butler had been chosen he would probably have remained leader of the Party for a long

122

time. Hailsham was not to Heath's taste or temperament as leader. But he liked Home; and Home, moreover, seemed unlikely to present any long-lasting obstacle to Heath's own ambitions, if only on grounds of age.

Having voted for Home, it was natural that he should accept office in his administration – unlike Macleod and Enoch Powell, who refused to serve. There and then Macleod also surrendered his co-chairmanship of the party. Lord Aldington, one of Heath's closest friends, who, after being deputy chairman, had become special assistant to the joint chairmen, Macleod and Poole, also decided to call it a day. So did Poole – but overnight he was persuaded to change his mind, on learning that the new Prime Minister intended to appoint John Hare chairman of the Party. Hare, who shortly afterwards became Lord Blakenham, was an old friend and the brother-in-law of Poole's business associate, Lord Cowdray. Poole therefore decided to stay on to assist him, assuming the rank of deputy chairman.

Macmillan has published his own version of this extraordinary episode. But the most arresting account of all – and no more arresting account is ever likely to be written – was provided by Iain Macleod. It appeared in the *Spectator*, of which he had become editor, on 17 January 1964. This was Macleod's rejoinder, intimately informed, outspoken and magisterial, to a book by Randolph Churchill, *The Fight for the Tory Leadership*.[13] I reproduce it in full, for it is one of the most remarkable political texts of the era, long unobtainable in print.

Until Mr Randolph Churchill's book appeared

ON THE SIDEWALK SUNDAY MORNING
LIES A BODY OOZING LIFE.
SOMEONE'S SNEAKING 'ROUND THE CORNER,
IS THE SOMEONE MAC THE KNIFE?

—"The Threepenny Opera"

17TH JANUARY, 1964: . . . IN WHICH HE STATES THAT MR. MACMILLAN WAS
DETERMINED THAT MR. BUTLER SHOULD NOT SUCCEED HIM

(*London Express News Service*)

there had been an unspoken agreement that the less said about the recent struggle for the Tory leadership the better. 'Macleod and Powell,' wrote a political commentator, 'have been reticent to a tactical fault.' The Prime Minister went out of his way to be uncommunicative on television and in his press interviews. With the exception of an intervention by Martin Redmayne, the Chief Whip, to which I refer later, little or nothing was said. Speculation, of course, was feverish, but with little to feed on soon died. The scars healed swiftly.

Four-fifths of Churchill's book could have been compiled by anyone with a pair of scissors, a pot of paste, and a built-in prejudice against Mr Butler and Sir William Haley. Its importance comes from the fact that this is Mr Macmillan's trailer for the screenplay of his memoirs. The preface includes the sentence: 'Wherever possible I have consulted the principal actors in this drama.' Originally Mr Churchill's preface said that he had been given full assistance by everyone except Mr Iain Macleod. This had to be altered. Among those who either haven't been asked for or have refused comment on this book are the Lord Chancellor, Mr Maudling, Mr Powell, Sir Edward Boyle, the Chief Whip, Lord Blakenham, Lord Aldington and myself. I do not imply that all or even any of those not mentioned did in fact help Churchill. I am sure that others also were not asked or, if asked, refused.

The attractive feature of the book is Churchill's enduring loyalty to and affection for Harold Macmillan. This flowers on the last page: '. . . the magnificent and heroic service – his last great service – that Mr Macmillan rendered to

125

the Monarchy, the nation and the Tory Party. From his sick bed, at the risk of his life. . . .' Churchill knows well (and acknowledges more than once in the book) that I share the loyalty and affection that he has for Macmillan. I was, I think, at the end perhaps the only member of Macmillan's Cabinet to hold steadily to the view that the Tory Party would do better under Macmillan's leadership at the polls than they would under any of the possible alternatives. Both of them then must know how much I would like to underwrite Churchill's conclusion in full. I cannot. And in so far as I can subscribe to the theory that Macmillan performed a signal service to the Tory Party, I can only do it by rejecting the basic assumptions of the book and arguing from the one premise that seems to me to offer a logical, defensible, and indeed honourable explanation of what happened.

Churchill writes: 'It can be argued that Macmillan did all he could during his seven years as Prime Minister to advance the fortunes of Butler.' Almost anything can no doubt be argued, but no one close to politics or to Harold Macmillan could seriously support this suggestion for a moment. The truth is that at all times, from the first day of his premiership to the last, Macmillan was determined that Butler, although incomparably the best qualified of the contenders, should not succeed him. Once this is accepted, all Macmillan's actions become at least explicable. He thought that three of the members of his Cabinet who were in the House of Commons, apart from Butler, were *papable* and of sufficient seniority to be considered: Maudling, Heath and myself. It was not by accident that he brought forward these three respectively to be Chancellor of the Exchequer, Minister in charge of our bid to enter the Common Market, Chairman of the Party and Leader of the House of Commons. He planned this and hoped that one of the three would show himself clearly as the future leader. It was not by accident that the three sessions of the much publicized and somewhat pointless planning weekend at Chequers on the modernization of Britain were presided over by the same three. Home, who left Chequers that very morning for an engagement abroad, was not even at the conference, and no one commented on his absence. Macmillan's private preference between the three of us is known to have varied, but when the time came it was clear that none of us had emerged with the necessary decisive lead.

Instead then of turning to Butler, who had enormously strengthened his claim with a performance of matchless skill in the handling of the closing stages of the Central African Federation, Macmillan, having scanned the Cabinet list, began, as Churchill records, to contemplate Hailsham. True, Macmillan had treated Hailsham with scant courtesy after the 1959 election, but Hailsham had always had (and still has) a strong hold on the affections of the right wing and of many key party workers. Unfortunately, as many thought and Marylebone confirmed (see also the significant difference in his figures in the *Daily Express* poll), he has no drawing power in the crucial central area of politics. And Butler has. Home at this stage and for some time to come had ruled himself out. Only Hailsham could stop Butler. And when Hailsham failed to gather enough support, then Macmillan still refused to accept Butler. He turned to Home.

The only interesting part of Churchill's book is the account of the advice Macmillan tendered: of how having first supported Hailsham in the decisive days, he switched to Home: of how he organized the collection of opinions by Lord Dilhorne, Lord St Aldwyn, Lord Poole, Mr John Morrison and Mr Martin Redmayne. Eight of the nine men mentioned in the last sentence went to Eton. Redmayne did not and it is appropriate to start by considering his role. He as Chief Whip had the key task. He discharged it with the dogged, agreeable blend of tenacity and loyalty with which he approaches all his chores.

It is important to consider to what and to whom the loyalty of a Chief Whip should be directed. Not, I think, to any individual. Nearly all appointments owe more to the advice of the Chief Whip than to that of any Minister. In recommending appointments or dismissals, no Chief Whip allows himself to be influenced by considerations of personal friendship. He must, if he is a faithful servant of the party, think first and last of the party. He, too, in the classic phrase, must be 'a good butcher'. It follows that if a Chief Whip becomes convinced that the Prime Minister is a major liability to the party he would be failing in his duty not to consider alternatives and, if need be, to press for change. Again, if as happened in this case, a Prime Minister has to resign, it is the duty of the Chief Whip to consider which man is 'best' for the party, and, if he comes to a clear conclusion, to do all in his power to achieve that result. Churchill wholly underestimates the significance of the fact that Redmayne believed that Home was the right man. His judgement may have been right or (as, of course, I believe) wrong. That it was sincere is beyond argument.

In a still higher sense, the same duty applies to an outgoing Prime Minister, and I can accept that Mr Macmillan discharged it with equal sincerity. He thought, and it is only honest to admit that many others shared his view, that Butler had not in him the steel that makes a Prime Minister, nor the inspiration that a Leader needs to pull his party through a fierce general election. I did not agree. That Butler is mystifying, complex and sometimes hard to approach I would concede. But, on the other hand, he has the priceless quality of being able to do any job better than you think he will, and of attracting to himself wide understanding support from many people outside the Tory Party. And without such an appeal no general election can be won.

The key day was Thursday, October 17, a day which for me began as an ordinary working day and ended with my firm decision that I could not serve in the Administration that I knew Lord Home was to be invited to form. The first indication that the day was going to be unusual came at breakfast. My wife came back from a long telephone conversation with one of our oldest friends (mainly concerning the affairs of a voluntary society in which they are both interested) to say that the succession was to be decided that afternoon. The information was third-hand, but the links were strong, and the original source the one man who would certainly know. I was surprised, but not disturbed. To me it seemed clear that if the situation was going to gell swiftly, the choice must be Butler: if there was deadlock, it would surely come back to the Cabinet. I had not, of course, appreciated then that it was in fact an essential part of the design that the Cabinet should have no such opportunity. Churchill's book makes this plain.

My only important engagement in the morning was a meeting at No. 10 called by Butler to consider the difficult closing stages of the Kenya conference. Both Maudling and I attended as ex-Secretaries of State for the Colonies. I walked away with Maudling to his rooms at the Treasury. I had always held Maudling in high and warm regard and throughout considered him a possible Prime Minister. Alone in the Chancellor's room over a drink I told him of my wife's telephone conversation. He had heard nothing, and had in general reached a similar conclusion to mine. Naturally his own chances (which he recognized were now slim) depended on the issue being protracted. A decision today, he thought, could only be for Butler. And with this he was more than content. He spoke on the telephone to Lord Dilhorne, and the Lord Chancellor confirmed that he and others were to present their collective views that afternoon. They had already been separately to see Macmillan that morning. To all suggestions that the Cabinet (or the Cabinet less the chief contenders) should meet, Dilhorne was deaf; as he had been, I have since learned, to at least one more similar request. No doubt he thought he was acting wisely.

Curiouser and curiouser it seemed, and Maudling and I decided to stay in touch. I joined him and Mrs Maudling for lunch. Butler we discussed a good deal. Hailsham we mentioned once, but we both knew that his bandwagon had long ago stopped rolling: indeed, the opposition to Hailsham (not, of course, on personal grounds) was and was known to be so formidable that it remains astonishing that he was not given clear warning of it in advance of his declaration that he would disclaim his peerage. Home we never mentioned in any connection. Neither of us thought he was a contender, although for a brief moment his star seemed to have flared at Blackpool. It is some measure of the tightness of the magic circle on this occasion that neither the Chancellor of the Exchequer nor the Leader of the House of Commons had any inkling of what was happening.

After lunch I returned to the Central Office to clear some papers. In mid-afternoon the telephone rang. It was an important figure in Fleet Street. He told me the decision had been made, and that it was for Home. He himself found this incredible, but he was utterly sure of his source. I telephoned Maudling and Powell and arranged to meet as soon as we could at my flat. Powell's views I knew coincided with mine and both at Blackpool and in the days following the conference we had been closely in touch. Almost at once the phone calls started from the leading newspaper political correspondents. Each of them had the same story. Someone, I presume, thought it proper even before the Prime Minister had resigned to prepare the press for the (unexpected) name that was to emerge. News management can be taken too far.

Before, however, any action could be contemplated, the story had to be confirmed beyond doubt. Maudling thought he knew someone who could clear this up, and he left us for half an hour. He telephoned back with confirmation and rejoined us, as did another member of the Cabinet. Lord Aldington also came to my flat and joined in our discussions. Meanwhile the stream of telephone calls from the press continued.

If we were going to make any serious protest against an invitation being extended to Lord Home, it was essential that he should know about this at the earliest moment. Powell and I each decided to speak to him direct. I had a dinner engagement myself, but telephoned Lord Home, who was out, and made an appointment for Powell and myself to see him after dinner.

From the beginning I was in no doubt that if, as Joint Chairman of the Party and Leader of the House of Commons, I felt strongly enough to tell Lord Home that I thought it wrong for him to accept an invitation to form an administration, I could not honourably serve with him in that administration. I slipped away for a moment to find my wife in her room. I told her what I thought the end might be, and yet that I felt clear that in the true interests of the Tory Party another point of view must be put. She agreed with me at once and has continued to back my decision through all the unpleasantness, local and national, that we knew we must face. Then my wife and I went off to the Political Committee's Dinner of the St Stephen's Club, where I made as gay and confident a speech as I could. After the dinner I telephoned Powell and went round to his house in South Eaton Place. When we telephoned Lord Home from there it was apparent that we could not see him without running the gauntlet of the reporters who had already encased him. So we spoke on the telephone.

I spoke first. I told him that there was no one in the party for whom I had more admiration and respect; that if he had been in the House of Commons he could perhaps have been the first choice; but I felt that those giving advice had grossly underestimated the difficulties of presenting the situation in a convincing way to the modern Tory Party. Unlike Hailsham, he was not a reluctant peer, and we were now proposing to admit that after twelve years of Tory government no one amongst the 363 members of the party in the House of Commons was acceptable as Prime Minister. I felt it more straightforward to put these views to him tonight rather than perhaps have to put them in other circumstances tomorrow.

I did not hear what Powell said to Lord Home, but I believe that he spoke to him on similar lines.

One by one the others, Maudling, Aldington and Erroll, joined us at Powell's house after their evening engagements. Thus came about the famous 'midnight' meeting. Churchill falls into the common error of assuming that only those events that were recorded happened. In fact, there were to my knowledge three meetings of Ministers that evening and there may well have been others. The reason this one was discovered was that Henry Fairlie, on telephoning the home of one of those attending it, was given a second number to try. This he traced as Enoch Powell's. Derek Marks, acting on a hunch that there might be a news story somewhere (and how right he was!), had decided to go and investigate for himself. He deserves whatever award there is for the scoop of the year. But that is to digress.

Shortly before Powell and I spoke to Lord Home, Hailsham had telephoned, having heard the report of the intended nomination of Lord Home, and he remained in close touch with one or other of those present during the rest of the evening.

Before long it was established that Maudling and Hailsham were not only opposed to Lord Home but believed Butler to be the right and obvious successor and would be ready and happy to serve under him. The rest of us felt this understanding between those hitherto the three principal contenders was of decisive importance: the succession was resolving itself in the right way. We telephoned the Chief Whip, who, rather than embark on a lengthy discussion over the line, decided to join us. He naturally did everything he could to persuade us to accept the situation as he saw it, but we finally asked him to report to the Prime Minister the fact of the understanding which had arisen between Butler, Maudling and Hailsham. He promised to do this.

Before the meeting ended, Powell and I, with Maudling, spoke to Butler himself, told him what had been agreed, and assured him of our support.

Next morning Churchill discovers a new '"Stop Home" movement, this time organized by Hailsham.' He is wrong. Hailsham didn't arrange the meeting between Butler, Maudling and Hailsham. I did. It is not true that 'Maudling failed to rally to Butler'. The meeting in effect was the logical outcome of what had happened the previous night.

But events were moving fast. Macmillan rallied Lord Home with the curious observation, 'Look, we can't change our view now. All the troops are on the starting line. Everything is arranged . . .', sent his letter of resignation to the Palace, and the same morning tendered advice to the Queen in the form of a memorandum which we are told incorporated all the four reports which Macmillan had asked for. So Churchill has it and his source should know. The memorandum then purported to be not the advice of one man, but the collective view of a party. There is no criticism whatever that can be made of the part played by the Crown. Presented with such a document, it was unthinkable even to consider asking for a second opinion. Nevertheless, the procedure which had been adopted opens up big issues for decision in the future. That everything was done in good faith I do not doubt – indeed, it is the theme of this review to demonstrate it – but the result of the methods used was contradiction and misrepresentation. I do not think it is a precedent which will be followed.

When Lord Home was sent for by the Queen and began inquiries to see whether he could form a government if he accepted her commission, Maudling and Hailsham kept to their agreement with Butler and declined to serve unless Butler did. Butler himself reserved his position, intimating that he would not serve under Lord Home unless satisfied that it was 'the only way to unite the party'. At this stage at least two members of the old Cabinet besides myself – Powell was one of them – who knew what the situation was, used their influence towards what they believed the right solution by answering Lord Home's inquiry in the negative. When, in the event, Butler decided to serve and Lord Home's government was formed, Powell thought it right to stand by the answer he had given.

I myself had two short interviews with Lord Home, one before and one after he became Prime Minister. Both were very friendly but brief. I am sure he would have liked me to change my mind. I like to think that he knew that I could not. For myself and for Powell it had become a matter of 'personal moral integrity'. The words are those of another member of the Cabinet.

When then *did* Home emerge as a contender? Hindsight is invaluable for politicians. People assure me now that 'everyone' knew for days or weeks or even years. In fact, the Cabinet left for Blackpool assured that Home was not a contender and that (if Macmillan's health failed) Hailsham probably was. On the Thursday I appeared on television with David Butler and listened to his appraisal of the contenders' chances. When he asked me afterwards (off screen) for comment, I said that it was a fine analysis and only obviously wrong in one assessment. I promised to tell him 'when all this is over' what was wrong. Lunching with him recently I explained my comment. Home, I told him, was at the time of the broadcast in no circumstances a contender. Nor, in spite of his own hedging television appearance, can he have been when he spoke on Friday to the National Union. Nor do I believe that to the mass meeting on Saturday he could have used these words, 'We choose our leader not for what he does at a party conference but because the leader we choose is in every respect

136

the whole man who is fit to lead the nation', if his own hat was already in the ring. On the Tuesday following Blackpool a member of the Cabinet came to see me. He had been trying without success to have a meeting of the Cabinet called to consider the situation. I gave him splendidly ironical advice in the light of what was already afoot. 'Try Alec,' I said, 'he's not a contender, and he ought to be a kingmaker.' He took my advice, but not surprisingly without result.

Although I am sure his friends were urging him to declare himself earlier, the explanation that seems least in conflict with the known facts is that sometime on Sunday or Monday – anyway, post-Blackpool – Lord Home began to organize his position.

On Friday, October 25, timing his speech to coincide with the opening of the Kinross campaign, the Chief Whip at Bournemouth set out to show that Lord Home was not a compromise candidate. Churchill (or rather Macmillan) by seeking to extend the argument to the other three groups brings the whole structure down in an absurd, even laughable welter of confusion. Home had formidable support. Much better to leave it at that. Any successful contender would have been a compromise selection. The account in Churchill's book therefore cannot be allowed to stand as history.

Redmayne said, and added, very properly, that some people would criticize him for revealing information given in confidence, that even on the first preferences Home had a very small lead. I am neither impressed nor surprised. The Chief Whip had been working hard for a week to secure the maximum support for Lord Home. So, quite properly, had several of the leading figures of the back benches. That in such circumstances Lord Home achieved a majority of one or perhaps two will amaze few people. And if the recording of opinions approached the confusion known to have been engendered by the method of sounding the Cabinet the margins of error must have been enormous. On the Third Programme Redmayne after repeating this went further. He said: 'The various sources of advice in greater or less degree came to the same conclusion.' One can at least be confident that this was so for the House of Lords. Churchill records: 'St Aldwyn was able to report that the peers were overwhelmingly for Home.' I'm sure they were. It reminds me of the verse composed in epitaph for Tom Harrisson who with Madge founded Mass Observation – Dr Gallup's forefather:

> They buried poor Tom Harrisson with his Mass Observer's badge
> And his notebooks: there were twenty thousand odd.
> And he'd not been gone a week when a report arrived for Madge:
> Heaven's 83.4 per cent pro God.

We are also solemnly told exactly what Field Marshal Viscount Montgomery thought and said. I would only comment that I personally would pay more attention on this issue to the views of a branch chairman of the Young Conservatives or of the Trade Unionist Advisory Committee than to those of Lord Montgomery.

The point of view of the constituency associations at Blackpool is put forward in Churchill's book as 60 per cent for Hailsham and 40 per cent for Butler. This doesn't seem to leave much for the rest of us and the spread was of course much wider. Then there is an involved explanation leading to the conclusion that only Home could avoid a split in the party. In another part of the book Churchill derides a *Daily Express* poll which produced the following result on Wednesday, October 16, in percentages:

	All Parties	Tories Only
Butler	39½	38
Hailsham	21½	27
Maudling	11	10½
Home	9½	10
Others and undecided	18½	14½

I believe in fact that this coincided closely with the actual figures. Churchill with a wealth of selective quotations tries to show how wrong the papers were. My account may do something to correct this. Most of the papers had a shrewd idea of what Ministers and MPs thought. In particular the lobby correspondents have been shown by events to have made a more accurate assessment of opinion in the Cabinet than the one attributed by Churchill's book to the Lord Chancellor.

For it is with the revelation of the Cabinet's opinions that we reach true absurdity. Not, I emphasize, as a matter of my personal opinion, but on the known and published facts. This first is Churchill's account. 'Dilhorne arrived at the hospital at 10.56 and he reported to the Prime Minister that most of the Cabinet were very strong for Home. Whereas originally there had been six adherents of Butler and six of Hailsham, Dilhorne had to report that the overwhelming consensus now pointed to Home. Home had the best chance of uniting the Cabinet if he could be persuaded to disclaim his peerage.' I cannot imagine what 'originally' means unless it is suggested that there were two or more polls by the Cabinet. On Friday, October 18, five members of the Cabinet met for a sandwich lunch. None thought Lord Home the first choice. Butler, Hailsham and Boyle were not present. That makes eight. Of the others I only know the point of view of five: two for Home, three for someone else. From my personal knowledge then, eleven were for candidates other than Lord Home and two in support. There were some half a dozen others. But even if there wasn't a single one of these for Butler or Maudling or Hailsham, the figures in the book (as other reviewers have pointed out) are simply impossible. How can one explain the inexplicable? William Rees-Mogg in the *Sunday Times* simply says that he 'declines to believe that Lord Dilhorne who behaved very properly throughout used the phrase "overwhelming consensus" or any similar phrase . . .' I think there must be another answer, if only because one can scarcely contemplate such a story being told with no foundation in fact. The answer must be that many Cabinet Ministers used words similar to those I used on the Thursday evening to Lord Home. And that the expressions of genuine regard for him somehow became translated into second or even first preferences.

There is of course much still to be told. Nevertheless what I have written does, I hope, enable the central drama to be seen in perspective. People inside and outside the Tory Party will assess the result in their own way. There will not ever be agreement as to which items should be assigned to the credit and which to the debit side of the ledger. I hold that the main conclusions are these. First, that there is real respect for the Prime Minister throughout the Tory Party. Second, that the Tory Party for the first time since Bonar Law is now being led from the right of centre. That this chimes with the wishes of many good Tories who were disturbed and angered by some aspects of our policies these last twelve years need not be doubted. Nor need it be doubted that there is anxiety among those Tories who believed most fiercely in those policies. Third, we are now on record as having rejected Mr Butler once more as a potential Prime Minister. Indeed we have confessed that the Tory Party could not find a Prime Minister in the House of Commons at all. Fourthly, we have gravely weakened the House of Lords. Not only by the departure of the two outstanding Conservative Ministers who were Peers, but because the long-term effect of the use to which the Peerage Act was put can only be to diminish the importance, even the relevance, of the hereditary principle.

I have argued that when the office of the leader of a great political party has to be filled it is wholly proper that all those who feel strongly should do their utmost to ensure that their view prevails. Such actions must sometimes cut across personal friendships. They need not destroy them. In this case I think they did not.

The decisive roles in the selection of Lord Home as Prime Minister were played by Macmillan and Redmayne. I am certain that they acted at each stage in the interest as they saw it of the sort of Tory Party in which they believe. So did I.

Chapter 10

If we accept Macleod's assertion that Macmillan was determined to deny Butler the succession, we are then bound to ask why, and with what justification. Butler's qualifications were surely self-evident and numerous. By virtue of experience, insight, intellect and parliamentary flair, he might reasonably have been thought the embodiment – the epitome – of statesmanship, with claims far exceeding those of Lord Home. Yet Macmillan was not convinced; and his resistance to Butler suggested – however mistakenly – a lack of generosity quite at variance with his reputation for good-natured, fair and tolerant instincts.

Macmillan and Butler were colleagues of many years' standing, with much in common, not least a scholarly turn of mind. They were similar in upbringing, in social outlook, in some of their intellectual (and even sporting) proclivities. Both were rich, established, assured. After serving together in successive governments, they knew each other pretty well.

Close political association had not resulted in the close personal friendship that might have been expected, however. Their relationship was scarcely more than a professional one – mutually comfortable, but never heightened by any marked warmth of feeling. While each has paid the other many a compliment over the years, in speech and print, and Macmillan as Prime Minister acknowledged his debt to Butler, there was a reserve between them, a distance. It is not easy to understand why.

One 'explanation' is that Macmillan mistrusted Butler because they were on opposite sides over Munich. As a young junior minister in Chamberlain's Government, Butler supported the Munich Agreement, while Macmillan, a rebellious backbencher, condemned it. But this alone will not do. If Macmillan disapproved of Butler for that reason, he could hardly have approved of Home, who was Chamberlain's PPS and actually accompanied him to Munich, or of Hailsham, ready defender of the agreement in the Oxford by-election of 1938. Yet Hailsham and Home were Macmillan's first and second favourites for the succession.

What is more likely, I think, is that Macmillan did resent Butler's lack of enthusiasm for the Suez adventure and categorized it as an extension – a further proof – of a deep-seated tendency towards 'appeasement' in the face of external provocation or aggression. Home and Hailsham may have been 'Munichites'; but, unlike Butler, they were strong for Suez. This counted with Macmillan. Again, we must remember that his contemptuous rejection of Chamberlain's so-called compact with Hitler was

143

rooted in the emotional ordeal of the First World War. In Hitler he had recognized a grave threat to peace – a threat that could be removed by timely action but not by conciliation. In a recent expression of his own, appeasement is the father of war. As a guardian of peace, Macmillan acknowledged the limited military intervention that might be necessary to preserve it. He dreaded a repetition of the sort of conflict that engulfed his own generation from 1914 to 1918. Butler, whom Macmillan evidently thought of as a contemporary, had not served in that war – if only because he was, in fact, slightly less than a contemporary and was eleven years of age at the outset. Yet Macmillan continued to *think* of him as a contemporary (or so it seems), but as one who had not undergone his own dreadful experiences – as if Butler had chosen to avoid them.

If these were some of the factors affecting his judgement, another may have been the reflection that Butler, as Prime Minister, might have succeeded in rivalling his own record both in achievement and durability. We are all familiar with this human tendency: it is that of the company chairman (or trade union leader or newspaper editor) who for the sake of contrast inclines towards a successor less gifted and perhaps less tenacious than himself. A lack of generosity is not a charge that Macmillan's record will sustain, although here and there one does encounter a failure of goodwill, a lapse from his normal benevolence and charity of mind. He was, let us say, unjust towards Anthony Nutting, one of the two ministers who resigned over Suez. The other was Edward Boyle, whom Macmillan restored to grace and government while leaving poor Nutting – perhaps the most distinguished of all the younger Conservatives of his day – in the political wilderness, to the party's detriment.

The grand Lord Salisbury, whose Elizabethan antecedents in the service of the State might alone have made him seem indispensable to any administration conducted by Harold Macmillan, met a similar eclipse (although he was very much older than Nutting) when, in the early months of the new Government, he challenged the Prime Minister's decision to release Archbishop Makarios from exile in the Seychelles. Makarios had been dismissed from Cyprus – transported – because of his involvement with Enosis, the movement for union with Greece. Macmillan and most members of the Cabinet, but not the magisterial Lord Salisbury, thought that he should be allowed to return, notwithstanding his complicity.

Salisbury protested in Cabinet, and then spoke to Macmillan alone in the small sitting room at No. 10. Macmillan was unyielding – whereupon Salisbury tendered his resignation. To his astonishment and indignation, it was at once accepted. As John Wyndham afterwards explained the Prime Minister's response: 'He did it because he thought that he would not be in office much longer and, while he was there, he was determined to show who was the boss.' Macmillan was upset, for he and Salisbury were old friends: yet there was no reconciliation. With Salisbury's resignation – or, rather, Macmillan's acceptance – the political influence of the Cecils was abruptly ended after four hundred years.

In contrast, Macmillan's attitude towards Peter Thorneycroft displayed the more generous – even indulgent – side of his nature. Two years after Thorneycroft's resignation as Chancellor, he was invited to rejoin the government, in which he

145

remained for the rest of its term, first as Minister of Aviation, finally as Secretary of State for Defence. In a totally different context, Macmillan showed the utmost consideration towards Oliver Poole after the latter's misfortune at the hands of Harold Wilson when in 1957 he was accused – quite wrongfully – of complicity in an alleged Bank Rate 'leak'. Poole, then deputy chairman of the Party, was completely exonerated by the Tribunal appointed under Lord Parker to investigate the charge, and Wilson duly discredited. In the result, and as if to compensate him for the peculiarly shabby smear to which he had been so recklessly subjected, Macmillan drew Poole into his confidence even more closely than before, and soon made him a peer.

Not all of Macmillan's personal friendships have been 'political', of course, or political in origin. Ronald Knox, who became a lifelong friend, was at once an intellectual companion and a spiritual influence. Harold Acton, with his palace near Florence, his devotion to the Arts and his great collection, is another far removed from the business of contemporary politics.

Nevertheless, Macmillan's close friends, his intimates, have tended to be more or less 'political', and usually of a rich patrician order, the owners of large estates, grand houses. Hence the so-called 'grouse moor' image, to my mind a most agreeable impression which he never thought of disguising. He liked shooting at Bolton Abbey with the Duke of Devonshire (although the present Duke does not himself shoot, he often accompanies the guns), just as he liked staying at Chatsworth. He was similarly at home with Lord Swinton at Masham (again for the grouse shooting), with John Wyndham at Petworth, with Lord Lansdowne at Bowood, with Lord Margadale (formerly John Morrison, chairman of the 1922 Committee) on the Isle of Islay, and with his brother-in-law James Stuart in the north of Scotland. Of these half-dozen friends, all Tories, four were members of his government, while Wyndham and Morrison, although not ministers, were among his closest political associates.

His shooting days are over now, of course, if only through failing eyesight, but he still pays occasional visits to Chatsworth and some of the other great houses that he has known so long, an ever-welcome guest, valued for the ease of his companionship, the radiance of his conversation and the perspicacity of his judgements on the passing scene.

In the House of Commons, friendships 'across the floor', between members of opposing parties, do of course exist, although they seem increasingly infrequent nowadays and often rest on little more than the mutual convenience of 'pairing'. It was neither exceptional nor surprising that Macmillan should have formed few friendships with members of the Labour Party. His pre-war association with such prominent figures as Hugh Dalton (and Dalton especially) was founded in rejection of Chamberlain's policy of appeasement, and strictly political rather than personal. Without the unifying influence of a great issue of principle, and in the more usual circumstances of party division, one would hardly expect close friendships to develop.

Nor did they. Macmillan never cared for Gaitskell – until he died. Upon his death he was at last possessed of a sense of Gaitskell's true quality and importance.

During the past few years, he has displayed a strikingly prophetic instinct for the political strains that have increasingly disturbed the country and derive from the growing assertiveness of the trade unions. He may have spoken colloquially, but he was speaking with insight and an accurate perception of what lay ahead, when he addressed these words to me in 1975 while discussing the theory of National Government:

> The only reason for a National Government would be to get a new deal, recognizing that having got political democracy we must have industrial democracy. It's either a new deal or a row. I have the feeling that the battle is not now between the parties. It's the old battle: Where does power reside? It's the old battle of the barons and the kings, the much longer struggle between the king and the church. What the church said is very much what the trade unions say: You can't tax us. Who is to be boss, the king or the church? Parliament is increasingly challenged by the bureaucracy, which is getting very strong, and by the trade unions. The trade unions run the present government. Sooner or later, this battle will come to an issue, which reduces the importance of the parties, so to speak. A paradox. What will Parliament do?

Without concluding that a National Government may ultimately result (or is to be desired), we can probably agree that events in the past year or two have amply fulfilled his essential prediction – his estimate – of the nature and the measure of the

148

developing conflict of interest which is so disrupting both our economy and our social cohesion as a nation. More widely, in his appreciation of European policy as reflected or represented by the Community, he is similarly anxious. In a broadcast with Professor Robert McKenzie to mark his eighty-fifth birthday, his reservations (intimated earlier) were bluntly expressed:

> Since it is purely an economic body or more or less a free trade area with a lot of bureaucratic system, we are getting all the troubles without any of the advantages. We argue about fish, about potatoes, about milk, on the periphery. But what is Europe really for? The countries of Europe, none of them anything but second-rate powers by themselves, can – if they get together – be a power in the world, an economic power, a power in foreign policy, a power in defence equal to either of the superpowers. We are in the position of the Greek city States: they fought one another and then fell victim to Alexander the Great and then to the Romans. Europe united could still, by not niggling about the size of lorries, but by having a single foreign policy, a single defence policy and a single economic policy, be equal to the great superpowers. For the moment, the future is very uncertain. Nobody is really facing this; nobody is coming out with this great demand, even the French or the Germans. Somebody must arise, somebody who, like Churchill, is not just an echo but a voice.

Had he been younger, he might (who knows?) have been able to develop that voice himself. In his 'European' – or internationalist – record there is

149

much to encourage the thought that he was capable of rising to the challenge and, partly by virtue of an engagingly persuasive personality as well as deep-seated convictions, to turn the Community firmly towards those larger ends. The passage of time has robbed him of the opportunity, however. Britain joined the EEC too late, and as a supplicant – a dilatory and handicapped recruit instead of an enthusiastic (and perhaps commanding) founder-member. Like newcomers to a club, we are lacking in seniority and authority.

On a more immediately domestic level, Macmillan has given Margaret Thatcher welcome and generous support, both publicly and privately, during the years since her election to the Conservative leadership in the winter of 1975. In economic outlook, they have been far apart in the past, the old expansionist, the new monetarist, the spender, the retrencher. Perhaps the distance between them is closing now. At all events they have more to unite than to divide them.

On a snowy day in January 1979 I attended an agreeably intimate little ceremony at the Carlton Club. In her presence, Macmillan was unveiling a head of Mrs Thatcher by Oscar Nemon. It had been commissioned by an elderly Canadian admirer of hers, Mr Harold Jackman, a former member of the Ottawa Parliament, and presented to the Conservative Party.

Macmillan was at his courtliest. Gazing round the drawing room of the club, he remarked on the number of portraits of past statesmen. 'I wonder what they would make of this performance', he said. 'I know one who would have welcomed it – Disraeli, who disliked the comany of men and liked the company of women.' Turning to contemporary politics, he became solemn, forseeing either a national revival under the Tories or, if Labour were again returned to office in the General Election, what he called a plunge to disaster. Addressing himself directly to Mrs Thatcher, he concluded: 'I wish you well with all my heart, madam. God bless you'.

With that, he took an armchair, and Mrs Thatcher, apparently quite comfortable on the floor, sat at his feet for half an hour. Four months later she fulfilled the first of his hopes.

References

1 *An Edwardian Summer* John S. Goodall (Macmillan, 1976)
2 *The Middle Way* Harold Macmillan (Macmillan, 1938; reissued 1966)
3 Vol. I, *Winds of Change 1914–1939* (Macmillan, 1966);
   Vol. II, *The Blast of War 1939–1945* (Macmillan, 1967);
   Vol. III, *Tides of Fortune 1945–1955* (Macmillan, 1969);
   Vol. IV, *Riding the Storm 1956–1959* (Macmillan, 1971);
   Vol. V, *Pointing the Way 1959–1961* (Macmillan, 1972);
   Vol. VI, *At the End of the Day 1961–1963* (Macmillan, 1973)
4 *The Past Masters: Politics and Politicians 1906–1939* (Macmillan, 1975)
5 Vol. I, *Winds of Change 1914–1939* (Macmillan, 1966)
6 *Ibid.*
7 *The Abuse of Power* James Margach (W. H. Allen, 1978)
8 *The Art of the Possible* R. A. Butler (Hamish Hamilton, 1971)
9 *Political Adventure* Viscount Kilmuir (Weidenfeld & Nicolson, 1964)
10 *Both Sides of the Hill* Lord Hill of Luton (Heinemann, 1964)
11 *The Other Revolution* Arianna Stassinopoulos (Michael Joseph, 1978)
12 *Wyndham and Children First* Lord Egremont (Macmillan, 1968)
13 *The Fight for the Tory Leadership* Randolph Churchill (Heinemann, 1964)

The author is also indebted to the *Spectator* for permission to reproduce the article by Iain Macleod in its entirety.

Index